TEENS & Race

HAL MARCOVITZ

THE GALLUP YOUTH SURVEY:

MAJOR ISSUES AND TRENDS

Teens and Alcohol

Teens and Family Issues

Teens and Race

Teens, Religion, and Values

Teens and Sex

Teens and Suicide

TEENS & Race

HAL MARCOVITZ

305.8

Produced by OTTN Publishing, Stockton, New Jersey

Mason Crest Publishers
370 Reed Road
Broomall, PA 19008
www.masoncrest.com

3 5 7 9 8 6 4 2

Library of Congress Cataloging-in-Publication Data

Marcovitz, Hal.
 Teens and race / Hal Marcovitz.
    p. cm. — (Gallup Youth Survey, major issues and trends)
Summary: Uses data from the Gallup Youth Survey and other sources to examine
issues related to teenagers' race and ethnicity.
Includes bibliographical references and index.
 ISBN 1-59084-721-0
1. Teenagers—United States—Attitudes—Juvenile literature. 2. United
States—Race relations—Juvenile literature. [1. Race relations. 2. Ethnic
relations.] I. Title. II. Series.
 HQ796.M279 2004
 305.8'00835—dc22
                                        2003018440

Contents

Introduction
George Gallup   6

America's Most
Diverse Generation   9

The Long Road
to Desegregation   17

Love in Black
and White   37

Growing up Biracial   49

When English Is Not Spoken   61

Young Muslims in America   77

Each Student Is an Individual   87

Glossary   102

Internet Resources   104

Further Reading   106

Index   107

Introduction

By George Gallup

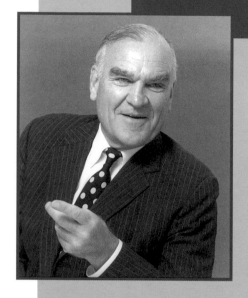

As the United States moves into the new century, there is a vital need for insight into what it means to be a young person in America. Today's teenagers—the so-called "Y Generation"—will be the leaders and shapers of the 21st century. The future direction of the United States is being determined now in their hearts and minds and actions. Yet how much do we as a society know about this important segment of the U.S. populace who have the potential to lift our nation to new levels of achievement and social health?

The nation's teen population will top 30 million by the year 2006, the highest number since 1975. Most of these teens will grow up to be responsible citizens and leaders. But some youths face very long odds against reaching adulthood physically safe, behaviorally sound, and economically self-supporting. The challenges presented to society by the less fortunate youth are enormous. To help meet these challenges it is essential to have an accurate picture of the present status of teenagers.

The Gallup Youth Survey—the oldest continuing survey of teenagers—exists to help society meet its responsibility to youth, as well as to inform and guide our leaders by probing the social and economic attitudes and behaviors of young people. With theories abounding about the views, lifestyles, and values of adolescents, the Gallup Youth Survey, through regular scientific measurements of teen themselves, serves as a sort of reality check.

We need to hear more clearly the voices of young people, and to help them better articulate their fears and their hopes. Our youth have much to share with their elders—is the older generation really listening? Is it carefully monitoring the hopes and fears of teenagers today? Failure to do so could result in severe social consequences.

Surveys reveal that the image of teens in the United States today is a negative one. Teens are frequently maligned, misunderstood, or simply ignored by their elders. Yet two decades of the Gallup Youth Survey have provided ample evidence of the very special qualities of the nation's youngsters. In fact, if our society is less racist, less sexist, less polluted, and more peace loving, we can in considerable measure thank our young people, who have been on the leading edge on these issues.

And the younger generation is not geared to greed: survey after survey has shown that teens have a keen interest in helping those people, especially in their own communities, who are less fortunate than themselves

Young people tell the Gallup Youth Survey that they are enthusiastic about helping others, and are willing to work for world peace and a healthy world. They feel positive about their schools and even more positive about their teachers. A large majority of American teenagers report that they are happy and excited about the future, feel very close to their families, are likely to marry, want to have children, are satisfied with their personal lives, and desire to reach the top of their chosen careers.

But young adults face many threats, so parents, guardians, and concerned adults must commit themselves to do everything possible to help tomorrow's parents, citizens, and leaders avoid or overcome risky behaviors so that they can move into the future with greater hope and understanding.

The Gallup Organization and the Gallup Youth Survey are enthusiastic about this partnership with Mason Crest Publishers. Through carefully and clearly written books on a variety of vital topics dealing with teens, Gallup Youth Survey statistics are presented in a way that gives new depth and meaning to the data. The focus of these books is a practical one—to provide readers with the statistics and solid information that they need to understand and to deal with each important topic.

* * *

Teens and Race offers a clear and objective account of the history of race relations in the U.S. and the long road to school desegregation, told in terms of Supreme Court rulings, events, and the struggle of individuals. This account provides the necessary perspective for the subsequent discussion in the book of current topics, including the challenges of growing up biracial; language issues related to the country's growing Hispanic population; treatment of Muslim youth in the U.S. in the aftermath of the September 11 terrorist attacks; and the debate over affirmative action programs.

The latest Gallup audit of black/white relations shows that 73 percent of whites feel that blacks are treated the same as whites in their communities, but only 39 percent of blacks share this view. For those who regard race relations as "the unfinished business of America," this book is vitally important reading.

Chapter One

The current generation of U.S. teenagers is the most racially diverse in the nation's history. In general, young people today are also more racially tolerant than any previous generation.

America's Most Diverse Generation

Today's teenagers are the most racially diverse group of young Americans in history. More of them are growing up in multiracial households than ever before. Opinion polls clearly show that young people today are more willing to accept members of other races as equals; they are eager to make friends with them, date them, sit in the same classrooms with them, share their music and other facets of their cultures, and ultimately, start families with them.

That does not mean that prejudice or racially motivated controversies have been eliminated in U.S. society. Decades after the civil rights movement of the 1960s, society still finds itself wrestling with such issues as cross-racial adoption, how best to serve non–English-speaking Americans, the violent and aggressive messages of hip-hop music, and whether colleges seeking to diversify their student bodies should consider a young person's race and ethnic background in the admissions process.

Perhaps one of the main reasons teenagers are tolerant of minorities is that today's young people represent the most racially mixed generation in U.S. history. According to the U.S. Census Bureau, the majority of people now living in mixed-race households are under the age of 18, meaning that many parents who are just now starting to have children are comfortable with the idea of marrying people of other races.

The Gallup Organization, a national opinion-polling firm, has long been interested in race relations, particularly among young people. Over the years, the Gallup Youth Survey, a long-term project by the organization to track the feelings and attitudes of young people, has often posed questions about race to American teenagers. In a poll of 500 teens conducted in 2001, 79 percent of teenagers told the Gallup Youth Survey they "feel comfortable being with people whose ideas, beliefs, and values are different from their own." Two years later, the Gallup Youth Survey polled 1,200 teenagers between the ages of 13 and 17 to find out whether race and ethnicity would influence their future choices for college roommates. Asked if they would prefer a white roommate, 68 percent of the respondents said it would make no difference; asked if they preferred a black roommate, 73 percent said it would make no difference, and asked if they would prefer a Hispanic roommate, 73 percent said it would not matter.

What Races Are Today's Teens?

What is the racial makeup of young people in America today? Although whites are still the dominant race in America, the 1990s saw some dramatic changes in the minority population of the United States. In 2000, the U.S. Census Bureau reported that blacks no longer make up the largest minority group in America. That status now belongs to Hispanics (also known as Latinos). The government attributed a large part of the growth in the Hispanic population to a wave of immigration from Latin American countries. The Census Bureau reported that fifty percent of the foreign-born population of the United States is from Latin American countries. For example, according to the Census Bureau, in 1970 the number of foreign-born U.S. citizens from Mexico was 800,000; by 2000 that number had risen to 7 million. Other Latin American nations responsible for the tremendous migration of immigrants into the United States include Cuba, the Dominican Republic, and El Salvador. "The proportion of the U.S. population that was foreign born reached an estimated 1 in 10 in 1997, the highest proportion since 1930," reported the Census Bureau.

The Census Bureau also found that the household size of the foreign-born population of the United States is larger than the typical household size of native-born Americans—when families immigrate to the

African Americans make up about 15.6 percent of the total population of Americans under age 18.

United States, they bring their children. Census Bureau statistics indicated the average household size for people who have emigrated from Latin America is 3.84, while the average household size for native-born Americans is 2.56.

According to the 2000 Census, the United States had a total population of 281,421,906, of which 274,595,678 people declared

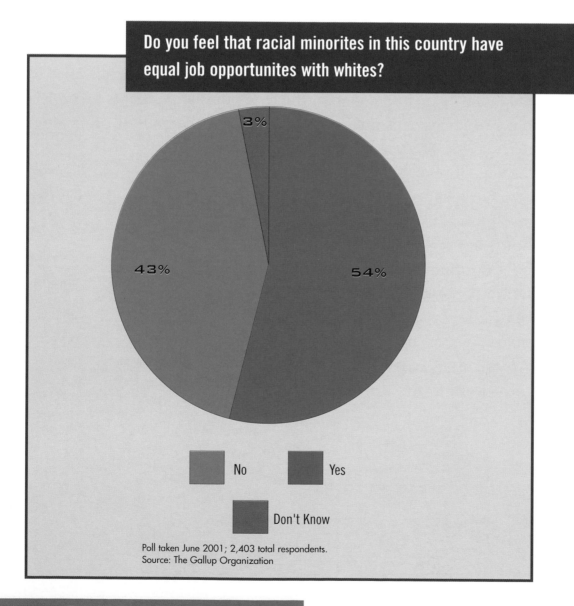

Do you feel that racial minorites in this country have equal job opportunites with whites?

3%

43%

54%

No   Yes

Don't Know

Poll taken June 2001; 2,403 total respondents.
Source: The Gallup Organization

themselves members of a single race. The number of single-race people under the age of 18 was recorded at 69,436,926—about 25 percent of the total U.S. population. A total of 6,826,228 people declared themselves under the Census Bureau's "Two or More Races" designation. That number included 2,856,886 people under the age of 18.

Based on the 2000 Census, the Census Bureau provides the following statistics on the number of people under age 18 in the United States who fall into the various racial and ethnic categories.

About 15.6 percent (10,885,696) of the total number of people under the age of 18 declared themselves to be black. The total number of blacks that year was 34,658,190, meaning that young blacks made up 31 percent of all African Americans.

In 2000, young Asians totaled 2,464,999, or about 3.6 percent of the number of people under 18 in America. Young Asians made up about 24 percent of the 10,242,998 Asians in the United States.

Young people who classified themselves as American Indians and Native Alaskans numbered 840,312, or just 1.2 percent of the total population of people under 18. According to the Census Bureau, there were 2,475,956 American Indians and Native Alaskans, meaning that young people make up 34 percent of the total of this group.

There were 127,179 young people in the Native Hawaiians and Other Pacific Islanders classification—just one-tenth of 1 percent of the total population of young people in America. Overall, there are 398,835 people in this racial group, which means young people make up about 32 percent of the total.

A total of 49,598,289 whites made up about 71.2 percent of people in America under age 18. With a total of 211,460,626 white

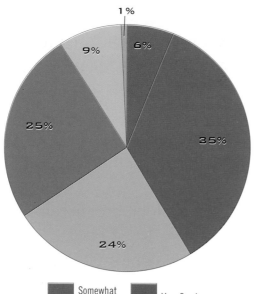

◀ **How would you rate the state of race relations in the United States today?**

Poll taken June 1998; 1,003 total respondents.
Source: The Gallup Organization

	Somewhat Good		Very Good
Neither Good nor Bad		Somewhat Bad
Don't Know		Very Bad

▶

Do you think public schools should offer classes on race relations as required instruction, should offer the classes as electives that are not required, or should not teach classes on race relations at all?

Poll taken August 1999; 1,029 total respondents.
Source: The Gallup Organization

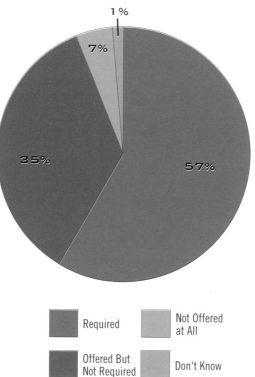

| | Required | | Not Offered at All |
| Offered But Not Required | | Don't Know |

people in America, young white people make up about 23 percent of the total.

According to the Census Bureau, there were 12,342,259 Latinos under the age of 18, or about 17.7 percent of the total of young people in the United States, in 2000. The total number of Latinos that year was 35,305,818, meaning that young people made up 35 percent of the total number of Hispanic Americans. It should be pointed out that while the U.S. Census Bureau does regard Latinos as a separate ethnic group, it does not regard them as a separate race. When people of Spanish or Hispanic backgrounds fill out their Census forms, they are advised to declare themselves members of whatever race in which they feel most closely associated. Therefore, the number of Latinos does not figure into the computation of racial makeup.

The Census Bureau permits people who do not feel they fit into any other category to declare themselves a member of "Some Other Race" when they fill out their census forms. Many people who declare themselves in this category could fit the definition of white or black, but for reasons that often have to do with pride of heritage do not regard themselves as members of those races. For example, the Census Bureau urges people of Middle Eastern descent to declare themselves white, but it is believed that many of those citizens do not regard themselves as white and, therefore, declare themselves to be Some Other Race on the census forms. In 2000, 5,520,451 people under the age of 18 were declared as part of the Some Other Race group, making up about 7.9 percent of the total number of young people in the United States. The Census Bureau reported that, overall, there were 15,359,073 people in the Some Other Race category, meaning that people under the age of 18 made up about 36 percent of the total.

Chapter Two

In 1954, the U.S. Supreme Court ruled in *Brown v. Board of Education of Topeka, Kansas*, that segregation in public schools was unconstitutional. However, fifty years after the landmark court ruling, many schools are not diverse.

The Long Road to Desegregation

Fifty years after the U.S. Supreme Court ruled in the 1954 *Brown v. Board of Education* case that racial segregation of schools was illegal, racial prejudice remains very much a part of life in America for many young people. Consider these cases:

Kenneth Chiu, a 17-year-old Taiwanese American student at Laguna Hills High School in California, was stabbed to death in the driveway of his family's home in the comfortable Los Angeles suburb. Police found an anti-Asian statement scratched into the Chiu family's car near where the dead boy's body was found.

* * *

A high school in Martinsville, Indiana, was prohibited from hosting sporting events in 1998 and 1999 because an angry white mob verbally assaulted visiting black basketball players from nearby Bloomington.

* * *

At Pennsylvania State University, 51 black students were asked to keep diaries over a two-week period as part of a school project on racism. A majority reported regular incidents of prejudice during the study. A typical complaint of the students was the refusal of white clerks at a local store to hand change directly to them; instead, the black students said, the clerks—many of whom were also Penn State students—preferred to place their money on the counter.

* * *

In Eugene, Oregon, a study of the city's mostly white schools "found that racism exists and may be on the increase." The report stressed "the frequency of racial jokes and slurs, derogatory racial stereotyping, and [less often] violent acts left unpunished by school authorities."

* * *

In Grand Junction, Colorado, 19-year-old Eric Valdez was stabbed to death after a white girl complained to her boyfriend that Valdez had flirted with her. During the fight that ensued, Valdez's assailant called him a "spic" and a "beaner," derogatory terms for Hispanic people. The boyfriend, 19-year-old Sjon Elmgreen, was charged with second-degree murder and ethnic intimidation.

Segregation in the United States

Prior to 1954, much of American society, especially in the southern states, was segregated. That was certainly true in the schools. There was a vast difference between the quality of education white children were receiving and the quality of education students could expect to find in "coloreds-only" schools. At the white schools, the buildings, textbooks, playground equipment, and even the chalk for the blackboards were often of good quality. At the black schools, the books were likely to be out of date, educational materials were scarce, and the facilities were often in need of repair.

Eleanor Holmes Norton, who would grow up to be a civil rights leader and member of Congress, recalled growing up in a segregated society in Washington, D.C., during the 1940s and 1950s. Even though her hometown was the nation's capital, it was still a southern city and its schools reflected the segregationist prejudices of the day. Norton recalled that, each fall, the teachers and students at Monroe Elementary School sat down with a stack of books and spent hours making them ready for the coming year's classes. Their job was to erase the pencil marks, mend the bindings, and make new covers for the books. The books were in need of repair because they had been used the year before at a whites-only school in Washington. Now that the white students were getting new books, the old books went to the black students. "You were reminded from the time you were a little child that you were in a segregated world, so deal with it," says Norton.

Southern blacks and other minorities had to endure such school conditions because of an 1896 decision by the U.S. Supreme Court in the case *Plessy v. Ferguson*. In that case, a black train passenger sued a railroad company after he was denied a berth in a whites-only sleeping car. The nation's highest court ruled that although the railroad had no responsibility to provide a black passenger with a berth in a whites-only car, under law it had to make sure a blacks-only sleeping car was available. That is how the doctrine of "separate but equal" originated. With this decision segregationists, particularly in the southern states, had legal precedent on their side: blacks could be separated from whites as long as equal facilities were made available to them.

Though in the South facilities for blacks and whites were kept separate, they were rarely equal. Over time, it became clear that areas of hotels, restaurants, movie theaters, and other public facilities reserved for whites were of much higher quality than what blacks had available to them. This was particularly true in the schools.

In 1938, the U.S. Supreme Court took up the issue again when it ruled that the quality of education provided to blacks at the University of Missouri was not equal to what whites could expect, because the college would not admit blacks to its law school and had no separate law school for them. This case represented a victory for African-American students, because it showed that schools were not adhering to the separate but equal doctrine handed down in the *Plessy v. Ferguson* decision.

The most significant test to the separate but equal policy was brought against the Board of Education of Topeka, Kansas, by the parents of Linda Brown, an eight-year-old black girl. Lawyers for Linda Brown's parents argued that the education the girl was receiving at a segregated school was far inferior to the education white students in Topeka could expect at their schools. The Browns' lawyers, who included future U.S. Supreme Court justice Thurgood Marshall, received help in making their case by the U.S. government. President Dwight D. Eisenhower assigned his attorney general, Herbert Brownell, to argue against racial discrimination before the Supreme Court.

The Supreme Court handed down its decision in May 1954, ruling unanimously that the separate but equal doctrine was unconstitutional. It ordered the desegregation of U.S. schools "with all deliberate speed." And, because the federal government had argued for Linda Brown's side, this decision meant that the resources of the federal government could be expected to help enforce the court's order. As it turned out, government intervention was necessary. Southern states were much opposed to desegregating their schools, and it soon became evident that U.S. marshals, as well as federal troops, would have to be sent to the South to make sure the Supreme Court's order was carried out.

The first test of desegregation occurred in 1957 in Little Rock, Arkansas, where nine black students attempted to enroll in all-white Central High School. Before the black students could enter the building, Arkansas Governor Orval Faubus sent the Arkansas National Guard to Little Rock. Faubus argued that troops were needed to maintain law and order, but their real mission was to keep the black students out of Central High School. For 18 days, Faubus and the Arkansas National Guard succeeded.

At first, President Eisenhower tried to use diplomacy to convince Faubus to withdraw the National Guard. When the Arkansas governor refused the president's pleas to desegregate the school, Eisenhower responded by using his authority under the U.S. Constitution to federalize the Arkansas National Guard, bringing the troops under his control as commander in chief of all American armed forces. Eisenhower ordered the National Guard to leave Little Rock, and then dispatched regular U.S. Army troops to Central High to ensure the black students could enroll. The soldiers would also guarantee their safety.

National guardsmen help an African-American student with his bicycle while enforcing segregation of Central High School in Little Rock, Arkansas, 1957. In September federal troops escorted nine black students into the school.

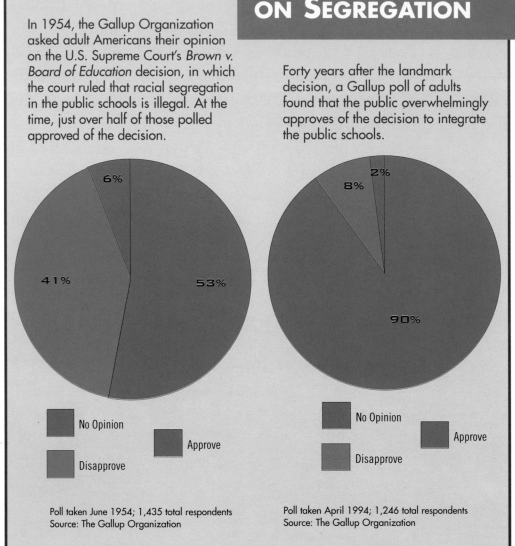

In 1954, the Gallup Organization asked adult Americans their opinion on the U.S. Supreme Court's *Brown v. Board of Education* decision, in which the court ruled that racial segregation in the public schools is illegal. At the time, just over half of those polled approved of the decision.

Forty years after the landmark decision, a Gallup poll of adults found that the public overwhelmingly approves of the decision to integrate the public schools.

6%

41%

53%

2%

8%

90%

No Opinion

Approve

Disapprove

No Opinion

Approve

Disapprove

Poll taken June 1954; 1,435 total respondents
Source: The Gallup Organization

Poll taken April 1994; 1,246 total respondents
Source: The Gallup Organization

On September 25, 1957, the nine black students entered Central High. Federal troops escorted them past an angry mob of whites, which had gathered to threaten the black children as they entered school. Violence soon broke out in the crowd, as angry demonstrators turned on news reporters, beating several of them. Black news reporters were singled out. So was the staff of *Life* magazine, which had editorialized in favor of desegregation. "The local police were not able to hold back the mob," recalled Elizabeth Eckford, one of the nine black students who enrolled in Central High. "By that time, the mob had grown to 1,000 people and they were about to get into the school. Police took us out of town for our own protection."

A History of Prejudice

Blacks were not the only minority group that faced racial prejudice in the United States. Starting in the 1870s, people from China began immigrating to the west coast of the United States, lured by the promise of jobs in the farm fields. Within a decade, there were so many Chinese immigrants at work in California and other western states that Congress felt compelled to pass laws limiting Chinese immigration.

Soon, the Chinese laborers were replaced by Japanese immigrants. In 1924, Congress limited Japanese immigration as well. By then, relations between the United States and Japan had grown testy over trade issues. Over the next two decades, as relations between the two countries deteriorated further, Japanese Americans were eyed with suspicion by whites. When Japan launched the surprise attack on the U.S. Navy base at Pearl Harbor, Hawaii, on December 7, 1941, touching off U.S. involvement in World War II, hatred for people of Japanese descent manifested itself in one of the ugliest chapters of American history. On February 19, 1942, President Franklin Roosevelt signed Executive Order 9066, permitting the military to take into custody, without regard to due process or their other legal rights guaranteed under the Constitution, anyone suspected of assisting Germany, Japan, and other enemy nations. Roosevelt's order led to the establish-

Racism against Asians, particularly Chinese immigrants, was common in the United States during the 19th century. This offensive cartoon, which appeared in a San Francisco newspaper in 1882, attributes social problems such as immorality and disease to Chinese immigrants.

ment of internment camps. Some 120,000 Japanese Americans were forced to wait out the war in these camps because the federal government feared they could be spies or saboteurs for Japan for no other reason than that they had Japanese ancestors.

Latinos felt prejudice as well, mostly due to America's often-strained relationships with Latin American countries and Spanish-speaking people. The United States had gone to war against Mexico in the 1840s, then fought the Spanish-American War in

1898. In 1916, bandits under the command of Mexican rebel leader Pancho Villa crossed over into the United States and raided the New Mexico town of Columbus, killing 17 Americans. President Woodrow Wilson responded by dispatching the American military into Mexico to track down Villa, but an extensive search for the bandits proved futile.

By the 1940s, whites in Los Angeles regarded the immigration of Mexicans with bitter feelings. On June 3, 1943, relations turned violent when the "Zoot-Suit Riots" (so named because of the flashy clothes, known as zoot-suits, worn by young Mexican men) erupted in Los Angeles. The riots started after Los Angeles police raided a Mexican neighborhood; newspaper reports of the raid stirred up emotions, leading to a demonstration staged by thousands of whites on downtown Los Angeles streets. Many of the demonstrators were soldiers and sailors home on leave. Marching through the streets of Los Angeles, the mob attacked every Mexican they could find. The mobs entered movie theaters and dragged hapless Mexican youths into the streets where they were beaten up. Al Waxman, editor of the *Eastside Journal*, wrote an eyewitness account of one of the attacks:

> At Twelfth and Central I came upon a scene that will long live in my memory. . . . Four boys came out of a pool hall. They were wearing the zoot-suits that have become the symbol of a fighting flag. Police ordered them into arrest cars. One refused. He asked, "Why am I being arrested?" The police officer answered with three swift blows of the night-stick across the boy's head and he went down. As he sprawled, he was kicked in the face. Police had difficulty loading his body into the vehicle because he was one-legged and wore a wooden limb.

Changing Attitudes

In 1960, four African-American college students sat down at a Woolworth's lunch counter in Greensboro, North Carolina. The establishment refused to serve blacks, so the students were told to leave. The black students refused, causing a scene to protest the discriminatory policy of the lunch counter. This protest, called a sit-in, drew national attention and prompted other African-Americans to stage demonstrations elsewhere. Sympathetic whites sometimes joined these demonstration. By the end of 1960, it was estimated that approximately 70,000 high school and college students had staged sit-ins at restaurants, movie theaters, public swimming pools, and other facilities that remained segregated despite the 1954 *Brown v. Board of Education* decision.

Still, schools seemed the slowest of the public's institutions to respond to change. In 1962, black student James Meredith attempted to enroll at the whites-only University of Mississippi. To guarantee that Meredith be granted admission to the college, President John F. Kennedy sent U.S. marshals to escort Meredith onto campus. They were met by an angry mob that pelted them with eggs, rocks, and bottles. Rioting ensued on the campus. When it became clear that Mississippi Governor Ross Barnett had no intention of putting down the riots, Kennedy sent 25,000 U.S. Army troops to the campus. Meanwhile, the marshals made sure Meredith could register and that he got to classes safely.

Eight months later, Kennedy again had to send federal troops to a southern college. This time, he dispatched troops to the University of Alabama, where Governor George Wallace vowed to bar entry to the campus by two black students, Vivian Malone and James Hood, who sought to enroll there. Wallace personally stood in the doorway of the registration building and moved only when ordered to step aside by the commander of the Alabama National Guard, which had been federalized by President Kennedy. After delivering a short speech denouncing "the trend toward military dictatorship," Wallace stepped aside, and the University of Alabama was opened to black enrollment.

Although many schools were desegregated during the 1960s, it was clear that educational opportunities for blacks and whites still were not equal. Black and Hispanic families tended to live in decaying urban neighborhoods; their children attended schools that were old and in need of repair, and their classroom equipment and textbooks were often outdated. Whites tended to live in newer sections of the cities; their schools had been constructed more recently. Many affluent whites had fled the cities for the suburbs; their taxes funded schools that were far superior to what city residents could expect.

A policeman speaks with African-American protesters during a sit-in at a "whites only" lunch counter. During the late 1950s and early 1960s, protests like this one drew national attention to the goals of the civil rights movement.

Governor George Wallace (left, flanked by uniformed men) stands in a doorway at the University of Alabama in order to prevent two African-American students from entering, 1963. Wallace had run for governor with the slogan "Segregation Forever." Pressure from the federal government ultimately forced the school to integrate.

The Post–Civil Rights Movement

In 1970, a federal judge in North Carolina thought he had the answer to educational inequity when he ordered black students bused to white schools and white students bused to black schools. Other judges followed his lead, and in 1971 the U.S. Supreme Court ruled that busing was constitutional and could be used as a method to ensure integration of the schools.

Those legal decisions led to massive protests by white parents. One notable example occurred in Boston, Massachusetts. In 1974, Judge Arthur Garrity ruled that Boston school officials were intentionally keeping the city's schools segregated and were forcing blacks to attend the oldest, most overcrowded, and most poorly staffed schools. He ordered the busing of 17,000 Boston schoolchildren to desegregate the schools. Most white parents refused to let their children be bused; on the first day of school in the fall of 1974, approximately 90 percent of white children stayed home from classes. Angry whites threw stones at black students when they tried to board buses to return home. A month later, 450 National Guard troops had to be sent to Hyde Park High School in Boston to keep order when a white student was stabbed by a black student. Another 500 troops were sent to South Boston High when an angry white mob surrounded the school after a similar stabbing incident.

Over the next several months, whites in Boston staged numerous protests. Anti-busing parades were held on city streets; often, local government leaders who had been charged with enforcing Judge Garrity's order led these parades. By 1976, it was estimated that some 20,000 white Boston students had left the city's public schools, enrolled by their parents in private or parochial schools. As a result, by the late 1970s, black students were now in the majority in the city's schools. In 1987, Boston city's schools were finally released from Judge Garrity's court order. By then, Boston school officials had implemented a voluntary school desegregation plan that enabled students to attend the schools of their choice within certain city zones. The plan was regarded as 80 percent effective in desegregating Boston schools.

Parents who moved to suburbs feared their students could be bused into city schools to help correct racial imbalances. However, in 1974 the U.S. Supreme Court ruled in *Milliken v. Bradley* that a suburban school district could not be forced to help correct a racial

Many minorities live in urban communities where schools are not as well funded as those in more-affluent suburban areas. As a result there is a difference between the educations of whites and of minorities. The dropout rate for blacks (13 percent) and Hispanics born in the United States (15 percent) is higher than that of white students (11 percent). In addition, according to recent data the average SAT scores of African-American students (430 verbal, 427 math) is approximately 100 points lower than the average score for white students (527 verbal, 533 math).

imbalance in a nearby city's schools. That decision also ensured that the only way a minority student could enroll in a suburban school district was to become a resident of that school district.

In 2001, researchers at Harvard University wanted to find out how far American schools had come since the 1954 *Brown v. Board of Education* decision and the Civil Rights movement of the 1960s.

They concluded that schools remain largely segregated. Among the findings of the Harvard study were that 70 percent of the nation's black students attend schools in which a majority of the students are black, and 36 percent of black students attend schools in which the black enrollment is at least 90 percent. "The proportion of black students in such schools has been rising consistently since 1986, when it was at a low point of 32.5 percent," the study said.

Hispanic students experience similar segregation. The Harvard researchers found that 36.6 percent of Hispanic students attend schools with minority enrollments, an increase of 13.5 percent since 1968.

For the most part, white students are the most segregated from other races. "Whites on average attend schools where more than 80 percent of the students are white and less than 20 percent of the students are from all other races and ethnic groups combined," the Harvard study reported. Even in Washington, D.C., a city with a predominantly black population, the Harvard study found that white students attended classes in which they were the majority. The study found that when the races do mix, it is usually the blacks and Hispanics that are mixed.

"Our research consistently shows that schools are becoming increasingly segregated and are offering students vastly unequal educational opportunities," said Gary Orfield, the Harvard professor who headed the study.

The Harvard researchers found a very simple reason for the continued segregation of American schools: Whites tend to live in white neighborhoods, blacks tend to live in black neighborhoods, and Hispanics tend to live in Hispanic neighborhoods. Over the years, legislators and judges have attempted to tackle the issue of how to desegregate the schools, but those efforts have largely failed due to community reaction, such as protests over busing, and constitutional issues like the *Milliken* decision. And so families that can afford to live in affluent neighborhoods send their children to schools in those neighborhoods, schools that usually have better books, computers, gymnasium equipment, and cafeteria food than schools in poorer neighborhoods. The Harvard study continued:

> Segregation by race is very strongly related to segregation by class and income. . . . Racially segregated schools—for all groups except whites—are almost always schools with high concentrations of poverty. Almost nine-tenths of segregated African-American and Latino schools experience concentrated poverty. The average black and Latino student attends a school with more than twice as many poor classmates than the average white student. . . . Poverty levels are strongly related to school test score averages and many kinds of educational inequality.

It would be wrong to say that the federal government has not been aware of the racial imbalance in American schools. Many studies by the U.S. Department of Education have pointed out that schools should be doing more to encourage diversity in the classrooms. "The racial and ethnic composition of the student population contributes to the linguistic and cultural diversity of the nation's elementary and secondary schools," said a 1998 report by the Department of Education. "Along with this diversity comes new learning opportunities for students and new challenges for schools to accommodate the needs of a diverse student body."

RACIAL PROFILING

One night in Dorchester, Massachusetts, two African-American brothers were walking home one night when a police car suddenly stopped and ordered the boys to halt. "You have any contraband?" a policeman shouted from the car.

"No," replied 15-year-old Joshua Richardson, the younger of the brothers.

The officer and his partner, both white, then left the cruiser and ordered the boys to stand against a wall, arms outstretched. When they searched the boys, the policemen did not find drugs, weapons, or other illegal items. After finishing the search, they told the boys to go home.

What happened to the Richardsons is an example of what is known as "racial profiling." The boys were stopped and searched for no reason other than that their skin color raised the suspicions of the white policemen. "If you got braids, a hoodie, and baggy jeans in my neighborhood, the cops are gonna be after you," Joshua later told news reporters.

Racial profiling surfaced as a national scandal in 1998, after two New Jersey state policemen shot and wounded three of four unarmed black and Latino men traveling in a van they had stopped. The men's attorneys proved in court that nothing about the van or the way it had been driven should have raised suspicions. The attorneys argued that the state troopers were likely to pull over blacks and Latinos, even when they had not done anything wrong, because they believed blacks and Latinos were more likely to be guilty of crimes. The victims of the shooting ultimately were granted a $12 million settlement.

Soon, cases of racial profiling surfaced in other states as well. Many blacks and Latinos stepped forward to tell stories of driving down a highway or city street and suddenly becoming aware that a police cruiser was following them. Eventually, the police would order their cars to stop.

Racial profiling is not limited to adults who drive cars. In Boston, an organization known as Teen Empowerment surveyed 300 black and Latino teenagers about racial profiling. The survey indicated that 210 of the teenagers reported being stopped or searched by police "without reason."

It is difficult to find proponents of racial profiling. State and city police officials claim there are no written or unwritten policies in their departments to conduct searches based on race. Police officials insist that when racial profiling occurs, it is done because the individual officer harbors prejudices based on his own experiences with minority offenders.

Statistics *do* suggest why white police officers might be prone to suspect blacks—particularly young blacks. According to a 1997 study of prison populations by the U.S. Justice Department, 60 percent of offenders under the age

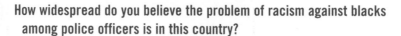

How widespread do you believe the problem of racism against blacks among police officers is in this country?

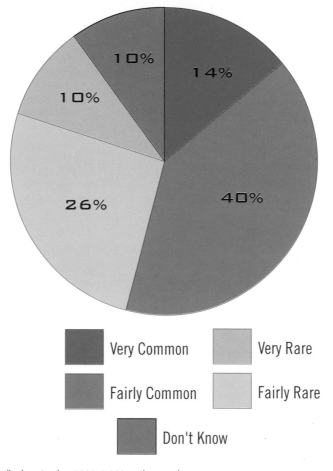

Very Common   Very Rare

Fairly Common   Fairly Rare

Don't Know

Poll taken October 1995; 1,223 total respondents.
Source: The Gallup Organization

of 18 sentenced to state prison terms are black. The study also found that 19 percent of young sentenced offenders are white, 13 percent are Latino, and 8 percent are from other races. Still, University of Toledo law professor David Harris, an authority on racial profiling, says that relying on statistics is an unfair way to draw conclusions about a class of people. "Is it true that African-

Americans are arrested and jailed disproportionate to their numbers in the population? Yes, that is true. That's a very unpleasant fact but it's a fact nonetheless," Harris says. "The thing is, you cannot draw from that that it makes sense to then stop all the African Americans or high percentages of African Americans or Latinos that you run into because even if there is more criminal involvement . . . the vast majority of these people are innocent, hard-working, tax-paying, right-living citizens."

To combat racial profiling, some states have passed laws requiring police officers to report racial data for every traffic or pedestrian stop and search they make. The reason for these laws is that if a particular policeman's reports show a tendency to search minorities, that officer might be practicing racial profiling. North Carolina, Maryland, New Jersey, California, Florida, and Ohio are among the states that have adopted such laws.

Opponents argue, though, that collecting racial statistics may not be the answer. They point out that police officers assigned to beats in black neighborhoods would, of course, produce reports showing an abundance of searches that involve black suspects.

Shortly after the terrorist attacks of September 2001, Muslim Americans complained they were being singled out for racial profiling. The administration of President George W. Bush promised to study the issue. In June 2003, the Justice Department issued a directive banning racial profiling by the 70 agencies of the federal government with police powers. The directive covers 120,000 law enforcement officers who work for the Federal Bureau of Investigation, Drug Enforcement Agency, Homeland Security Department, Bureau of Alcohol, Tobacco and Firearms, and other agencies. "Religious or ethnic or racial stereotyping is simply not good policing," said Assistant Attorney General for Civil Rights Ralph Boyd. "We want to make sure it doesn't happen, even once."

While the Justice Department's directive covers federal agencies, state and city governments are still responsible for the activities of local police departments. The American Civil Liberties Union says some local governments have been slow to outlaw racial profiling. In 2003, the ACLU filed a lawsuit against the city of Charleston, West Virginia, alleging that three black college students were racially profiled by police officers who ordered them out of their car, handcuffed them, then interrogated and searched the students for an hour before releasing them. It is obvious that the issue of racial profiling, like the larger problem of discrimination, is one that will not disappear overnight.

Chapter Three

Interracial relationships are more common today than at any time in past U.S. history. Approximately three-quarters of teens feel that interracial dating is "no big deal."

Love in Black and White

Randolph County High School, located in Wedowee, Alabama, is not unlike many public schools in the South. Although the U.S. Supreme Court ordered schools to desegregate in 1954, in many southern cities and towns school administrators were slow to carry out the court's wishes. It was not until well into the 1960s—and even the 1970s in some cases—for the old "separate but equal" idea to finally die. By the 1990s, blacks and whites in the United States were sitting in the same classrooms, using the same textbooks, riding together on the same school buses, and eating in the same school cafeterias.

But at some southern schools, there have been other, less obvious ways in which the races remained separated. For example, even today some southern schools continue to elect separate class officers—blacks get to vote for black officers, whites vote for white officers. Homecoming kings and queens are often elected along racial lines. And in some schools, whites and blacks hold separate proms. This was not the case at Randolph County High School. The school has about 2,200 students, about a third of whom are black. The 1994 prom was planned to be interracial; all students, regardless of color, were invited to attend.

Nevertheless, in Wedowee, a town located deep in the rural South, old feelings about the separation of the races remained quite alive. Although the town had agreed to accept an interracial prom, attendance by interracial couples was another matter. So when 16-year-old ReVonda Bowen, who is black, mentioned to Randolph County High School Principal Hulond Humphries that she and her boyfriend, who was white, planned to attend the school prom, it set off a chain of events that would make Wedowee a center of national attention in the debate over race.

Early in 1994, when Bowen told Humphries she planned to attend the prom with her white boyfriend, the principal reportedly told her he would never allow this. According to Bowen, Humphries became so enraged at the idea that he told Bowen—the daughter of a black mother and white father—it had been a "mistake" for her parents to have children.

Those alleged comments by Principal Humphries set off a firestorm of protest in the black community. Many whites also called for his ouster as principal. The Randolph County School Board was forced to suspend Humphries. Bowen filed a federal lawsuit against the school district, alleging discriminatory practices and violations of the *Brown v. Board of Education* ruling. The U.S. Justice Department also opened an investigation into the Randolph County schools.

Things grew even worse as tempers flared and hostility grew on both sides of the issue. That summer, an arsonist burned down

Randolph County High School. The son of a black civil-rights leader in Wedowee was charged with the crime but acquitted by a jury. For a time, Humphries was forced to fend off public accusations that *he* had committed the arson.

Despite the unrest in Wedowee, the 1994 Randolph County High School prom was eventually held, and ReVonda Bowen did attend with her white boyfriend. But the sad story of Randolph County High School did not end with the 1994 prom or the fire that burned down the school. Harsh feelings dominated the community in the years that followed.

In late 1994, the Justice Department announced the findings of its investigation. It found that the hostility Principal Humphries allegedly showed to ReVonda Bowen was not an isolated incident. Federal investigators determined that school officials were guilty of disciplining black students more harshly than white students and that the school district had failed to recruit black teachers and other staff members.

School officials reached a settlement with Justice Department attorneys. Under the agreement, the Randolph County School Board agreed to suspend Humphries and bar him from setting foot inside any Randolph County school for three years, although the board was permitted to continue to employ Humphries in another capacity, which it decided to do. "We are not in the business of managing school districts, but we have a clear responsibility to ensure that existing barriers to equality of educational opportunities are eradicated," said Assistant U.S. Attorney General Deval L. Patrick, as he announced the court settlement with the Randolph County School Board.

Unfortunately, the settlement with the Justice Department did not put an end to the problems in Randolph County. The school board was forced to defend itself against ReVonda Bowen's lawsuit. The board reached an out-of-court settlement with the student, agreeing to create a $25,000 college scholarship fund for her.

Meanwhile, the high school had to be rebuilt. For two years, the students at Randolph County attended classes in mobile homes that had been converted into temporary classrooms, using books borrowed from neighboring school districts. The cost of rebuilding the school was so devastating to tiny Wedowee that the state government of Alabama was forced to help subsidize construction of the new school. Black and white students at Randolph County said it was difficult to put the incident behind them.

Humphries waited out his banishment, and in 1997 ran for the elective post of Randolph County school superintendent. He easily won the election, and this reopened old wounds. "He just treats white people and black people differently," commented Wedowee resident Deliah Knight. "And you know, if he's going to do that, he doesn't need to be in the schools." (Humphries served an uneventful term as school superintendent and retired in 2000.)

What happened in Wedowee was an extreme reaction to the idea that young people of different races should have the right to hold hands in public. At one time in the United States, a young black man who even looked at a white girl could find himself the victim of a lynch mob. The case of Emmett Till stands out among others. Till, a 14-year-old black from Chicago, Illinois, was afflicted with a speech impediment that caused him to whistle when he spoke. In 1955, while visiting family in Mississippi, he had the misfortune of trying to speak to a white girl. Till's comments to the girl were misinterpreted by white men as a wolf whistle; he was abducted and brutally murdered. His killers were acquitted by an all-white jury.

Young People's Thoughts on Interracial Dating

Today, Americans, particularly young Americans, are much more tolerant of interracial dating. In 1997, the Gallup Youth Survey asked 602 teenagers between the ages of 13 and 17 to

Maime Bradley, the mother of slain 14-year-old Emmett Till, weeps before a coffin containing his body. Till was visiting relatives in Mississippi in 1955 when he was murdered for speaking to a white woman. Two white men, Roy Bryant and J. W. Milam, were put on trial for the murder but were acquitted by an all-white jury. The Till case attracted national attention to the growing violence against African Americans in the South. "Two months ago I had a nice apartment in Chicago. I had a good job. I had a son," Maime Bradley told reporters. "When something happened to the Negroes in the South I said, 'That's their business, not mine.' Now I know how wrong I was. The murder of my son has shown me that what happens to any of us, anywhere in the world, had better be the business of us all."

To many people the term *interracial dating* refers to couples in which one partner is black and the other white. However, the term can refer to a wide range of racial relationship combinations.

express their thoughts on interracial dating. Seventy-three percent of the respondents said interracial dating was "no big deal." That level of tolerance among teens is higher than what the Gallup Organization has found among adults. In a 2002 poll, the Gallup Organization found that just 65 percent of adult respondents approve of interracial marriage.

Of course, young people are the best judges of their own feelings and attitudes. In interviews with news reporters, teenagers who date people of other races have said they often have difficulty convincing their parents to accept these relationships. "It was different for them," said Kiley S., a black teenager who said her parents were at first shocked when she brought home a new boyfriend, Matt W., who is white. Her parents soon learned to accept her relationship. "Now, they're just like, 'It's your choice, and we can only hope you make the best choice,'" she said. Kiley and Matt attended high school in Georgia, and Kiley said she often found people glancing at them whenever the couple went on a date. She admitted feeling uncomfortable with that type of scrutiny of their activities.

Another Georgia high school student, Jonathan M., who said he is of Hispanic descent, told a news reporter, "I dated a black girl for two and a half years. I think there is a lot of racial tension that goes with it. We stopped going to the mall because people would give us ugly looks. There was one time when we walked past a family, and the mother pulled her child away from us."

Opposition to interracial dating can also be found among teenagers. A Georgia teenager named April D., who has dated interracially, says not all young people are willing to accept interracial relationships. April says black girls are often hostile to white girls who date black boys because they feel the "white girls are crossing their territory and taking their men away."

Hostility toward interracial dating is not limited to any geographic region. In Phoenix, Arizona, a 17-year-old African-American named David H. and a 16-year-old white girl named Lauren K. told a reporter that an interracial couple with whom they were friends was relentlessly harassed by a bigoted student. David and Lauren told the reporter that the situation got so ugly that their friends were forced to reevaluate their relationship before deciding to tough it out and stay together. As for their own relationship, David said, "I never saw that she was white and I was black. I just saw Lauren." Added Lauren, "If you really care for a person, you should sacrifice all that you can for them, no matter what, because relationships are something definitely worth fighting for."

Teens involved in interracial relationships say they enjoy each other's company, having fun together, studying together, and helping each other through the problems and tangles of adolescence. In fact, there is some evidence to suggest that young people involved in interracial dating relationships have more fun than people who date only within their own race. Psychologists at the University of California studied that issue in 2002. They surveyed female college students at the school's Los Angeles and Pomona campuses. Sixty-four women participated in the survey, of which 31 were involved in same-race dating relationships, and 33 were involved in interracial relationships. The researchers asked the question: "How happy are you with the relationship?" The respondents were asked to rate their answers on a scale of 1 to 7, with 1 representing "not at all happy" and 7 representing "very happy." Women dating boyfriends of another race scored higher in the poll, with an average of 6.2, compared to an average of 5.7 for women dating boyfriends of the same race. "One possible explanation may be due to the fact that individuals in a mixed-ethnicity relationship automatically work harder on communicating and understanding each other in their relationship due to cultural differences that cannot be ignored," the study's authors wrote.

Not surprisingly, women in interracial relationships were more favorable to interracial dating than the women in same-race relationships. Asked to react to the statement "Inter-ethnic dating should be avoided," the women in interracial relationships scored a 1.3, indicating that they strongly disagreed with the statement. Women in same-race relationships also disagreed with the statement, but by a somewhat lesser margin; their average score on this question was 2.

Many interracial couples must work harder at communicating and understanding each other than same-race couples. However, the difficulties that interracial couples face may help them grow closer.

The Persistence of Discrimination

Even today, many schools in the United States continue to wrestle with segregation-related issues. An example is Taylor County High School, located in central Georgia. In 2003 the school was praised by civil rights activists when its first interracial prom was held. A year later, school administrators found themselves embarrassed to announce that some white students wanted to return to the old segregated ways.

Taylor County High has approximately 420 students, of which about half are black and half are white. For decades, the school held separate proms for blacks and whites. In 2002, though, student leaders in the junior class, which organizes the prom, asked administrators to hold one prom for everybody. "The kids got together," said Gerica M., a black student who originally suggested the interracial prom. "The students tore down the Berlin Wall. Both sides were tired of it." A highlight of the prom was the decision by the students to elect a white prom queen and black prom king.

However, despite the decision to stage a single prom, the school maintained some of its other segregated traditions — blacks and whites continued to elect separate class officers, for example. And the next year, white juniors at Taylor County High voted to hold their own prom and not invite blacks. That year, Gerica M. was a senior. When she heard that the white students planned their own prom, she said, "I cried. The black juniors said, 'Our prom is open to everyone. If you want to come, come.'"

White students who spoke with reporters defended the decision to hold a separate prom. Many said the decision was not based on race, just a desire to be among friends for an event they all considered a special part of their high school experiences.

Many white students said they planned to attend both proms. "I had some white friends who were not going to the other [inclusive] prom," said white senior Erin Posey. "I wanted to have some time with everybody. I'll have a lot of [black] friends there, too. A lot more of the seniors are going to be at the mixed one."

Civil rights activists looked at the situation at Taylor County High School and wondered why the message of racial equality did not seem to be getting through. "It just breaks my heart to know that, in this day and age, a form of racism this blatant could manifest itself," said Elaine Hatchett, a district coordinator for the Georgia chapter of the National Association for the Advancement of Colored People (NAACP). "We are in the year 2003, and these are the kinds of things we still have to contend with."

Chapter Four

Some teens may be confused about their "ethnic identity." Children of an interracial marriage may struggle to find a group of peers with whom they can identify.

Growing up Biracial

When people of different races date one another, some of them are going to fall in love, get married, and have children. As the children of biracial marriages grow into adolescents, they are faced with a fundamental question: What is *my* race?

That question is not often easily answered. As young children, the sons and daughters of biracial marriages often turn to their mothers and fathers to help them with the answers. Young biracial children know they are different from their friends, and they know their parents are different from their friends' parents. The easy answer many parents give to their child's question "What race am I?" is "Both." However, some parents do stress one race over the other. That attitude may be well intentioned, but often such attempts seem forced, or they tend to confuse a young child. For example, a white parent may seem out of place at a Kwanzaa celebration.

However parents choose to deal with the question, young children are likely to accept their explanation because young children are not yet ready to question their parents' advice and judgment. But teenagers are old enough to draw their own conclusions, and when they find themselves wondering whether they are black or white, or whether they are Asian or white, or black or Latino, or whatever, the answers their parents give them may no longer be satisfactory.

According to Mount Holyoke College psychology professor Beverly Daniel Tatum, who has written extensively on biracial families:

> During adolescence many biracial teens feel pressured to choose one racial group over another. As the school cafeteria becomes increasingly divided along racial lines, where does the biracial student choose to sit? If parents have encouraged black identification and the young person's physical appearance fits that identity, the initial choice may seem easy. But the narrow definition of blackness that black adolescents typically use may leave the black-identified child with a white parent feeling not quite black enough. Or if the adolescent is very light-skinned, black peers who do not know the individual's racial heritage may question his or her presence in their group.

The truth of the matter is that more and more adolescents find themselves with the dilemma of racial identification because more and more adolescents are growing up in biracial homes.

In 2000, the U.S. Census Bureau for the first time permitted people to designate themselves "Two or More Races" on their census forms. When all those Two or More Races forms were counted, the bureau announced that 6.8 million people, or about 2.4 percent of the total population of the United States, regarded themselves as biracial. Approximately 2.8 million people, or about 42 percent of the total, were reported by the census bureau to be under age 18. This means that young people represent the largest segment of the Two or More Races group. As for single-race people under 18, they formed 25 percent of their overall group. This means that the biracial population is growing at a faster pace than the population of single-race people.

There is no lack of role models for biracial young people. Athletes Derek Jeter of the New York Yankees and Dwayne Johnson (known to wrestling fans as The Rock) are the children of biracial parents. Pop stars Mariah Carey, Alicia Keys, Lenny Kravitz, Michelle Branch, Vicky Sue Robinson, and Mya are biracial. So are actors Vin Diesel, Rosario Dawson, and Halle Berry.

Person 1

Your answers are important! Every person in the Census counts.

1 **What is this person's name?** *Print the name of Person 1 from page 2.*
Last Name

First Name   MI

2 **What is this person's telephone number?** *We may contact this person if we don't understand an answer.*
Area Code + Number

3 **What is this person's sex?** *Mark* ☒ *ONE box.*
☐ Male
☐ Female

4 **What is this person's age and what is this person's date of birth?**
Age on April 1, 2000

Print numbers in boxes.
Month   Day   Year of birth

➡ **NOTE: Please answer BOTH Questions 5 and 6.**

5 **Is this person Spanish/Hispanic/Latino?** *Mark* ☒ *the* **"No"** *box if* **not** *Spanish/Hispanic/Latino.*
☐ **No,** not Spanish/Hispanic/Latino
☐ Yes, Mexican, Mexican Am., Chicano
☐ Yes, Puerto Rican
☐ Yes, Cuban
☐ Yes, other Spanish/Hispanic/Latino — *Print group.* ↗

6 **What is this person's race?** *Mark* ☒ *one or more races to indicate what this person considers himself/herself to be.*
☐ White
☐ Black, African Am., or Negro
☐ American Indian or Alaska Native — *Print name of enrolled or principal tribe.* ↗

☐ Asian Indian   ☐ Native Hawaiian
☐ Chinese   ☐ Guamanian or Chamorro
☐ Filipino
☐ Japanese   ☐ Samoan
☐ Korean   ☐ Other Pacific Islander — *Print race.* ↗
☐ Vietnamese
☐ Other Asian — *Print race.* ↗

☐ Some other race — *Print race.* ↗

7 **What is this person's marital status?**
☐ Now married
☐ Widowed
☐ Divorced
☐ Separated
☐ Never married

8 **a. At any time since February 1, 2000, has this person attended regular school or college?**
Include only nursery school or preschool, kindergarten, elementary school, and schooling which leads to a high school diploma or a college degree.
☐ No, has not attended since February 1 → *Skip to 9*
☐ Yes, public school, public college
☐ Yes, private school, private college

The 2000 U.S. Census was the first that permitted people to list themselves as "two or more races." According to census data, in 2000 about 2.8 million young people considered themselves members of two or more racial groups.

Changing Attitudes Toward Interracial Marriage

There is no question that interracial marriage is much more accepted now than in years past. Until 1967, many states had so-called anti-miscegenation laws—legal prohibitions against interracial marriage. Such statutes were holdovers of the old Jim Crow laws, which were passed in the southern states during the post–Civil War years; nevertheless, they stayed on the books over the decades and were occasionally enforced. One of the oldest

GETTING BACK MORE THAN YOU GIVE

In 1995, child welfare authorities in Phoenix, Arizona, discovered 10 Latino brothers and sisters living in squalor in a tiny apartment. Their mother, an alcoholic, would often leave them for days at a time. The 10 children had four different fathers, none of whom could be located by police. All 10 children were placed in foster care.

Soon Van and Shirley Hughes, a white couple, stepped forward and offered to adopt the entire family. All 10 children moved into the Hughes home. Despite the problems of trying to squeeze 10 children into a modest home, things seem to be working out for the family. "My mind told me, 'I'm 50 years old, what would I want 10 kids for at this age?'" recalled Van Hughes, a retired U.S. Navy chief. "But my heart told me it was the right thing to do." If the Hugheses had not stepped in, chances are the children would have been separated from each other. Social workers would have been forced to find adoptive parents willing only to take one or two of the children.

There have been some awkward moments and difficult times. Van and Shirley Hughes had been looking forward to early retirement and years of leisure, but the demands of raising 10 children have put those plans on hold. After leaving the Navy, Van Hughes took a job as a security guard to help make ends meet. To help ease the overcrowding, they added two bedrooms to their Mesa, Arizona, home. Money is tight. "We take it a day at a time," says Van Hughes. "I'm not a saint. I'm just a normal guy. You get so much more back than what you give."

anti-miscegenation laws on record was adopted in Virginia in 1691, when the state was still a colony of England. The law endured until 1967, when an interracial couple, Richard and Mildred Loving, won a decision by the U.S. Supreme Court overturning the Virginia anti-miscegenation law.

In 1958, Richard Loving, a white man, and his black fiancée, Mildred Jeter, lived in Caroline County, Virginia, but traveled 80 miles to Washington, D.C., to be married because in Virginia interracial marriage was illegal. After their wedding, they returned to Virginia and were eventually arrested. They were convicted of breaking the state's anti-miscegenation law and sentenced to a

While there is no question that the Hugheses provided a much-needed rescue for the children, sociologists worry that when white couples adopt children of another race, the children eventually lose their cultural identity. "The absence of an adult of color in the family to serve as a racial role model may make adolescent identity development more difficult," says psychologist Beverly Daniel Tatum. "In addition, the identity process is often complicated by the adolescent's questions and feelings about the adoption itself. 'Who are my biological parents? What were the circumstances of my birth? Why did my birth mother give me up for adoption?' These questions and the underlying feelings of rejection and abandonment add another layer to the complex process of identity development."

Writer Rose Martelli, who is white, recalled that her adopted brother Matt, who is black, had a difficult time adjusting when he joined her family in 1973. Martelli said there were few efforts to reinforce Matt's birth culture as he grew older. As an adult, Martelli says, her brother listens to white-oriented music and dates only white women. "My family was so oblivious to race, it makes me laugh now," Martelli wrote. "Every day after school, my siblings and I would catch reruns of 'Diff'rent Strokes'—the hit '80s sitcom about two black boys adopted by a wealthy white widower—yet none of us ever made the connection. My parents didn't push the subject, either. Matthew was usually the only black person wherever we went, but I can't recall a single family meeting to address his predicament."

year in prison, but the judge suspended the sentence if they promised to leave Virginia. The Lovings accepted the judge's offer and moved to Washington.

Six years later, Mildred Loving wrote to U.S. Attorney General Robert Kennedy and asked for his help to overturn Virginia's anti-miscegenation law. Kennedy said there was nothing he could do, but he urged her to contact the American Civil Liberties Union (ACLU). The Lovings took his advice. The ACLU accepted the case and filed a lawsuit against the state of Virginia. In 1967, the U.S. Supreme Court ruled that Virginia's law was unconstitutional. Bernard Cohen, the ACLU attorney who represented the Lovings, recalled Richard Loving's advice to him shortly before he argued the case before the nation's highest court. "He was very country, sort of rough," Cohen said. "He just said, 'Tell them I don't understand why if a man loves a woman he can't marry her no matter what her color.'"

Despite the court's ruling, some southern state legislatures kept their anti-miscegenation laws on the books as symbolic gestures, knowing they could not be enforced. Over the years, however, all of the archaic laws were eventually repealed. The last state to hold onto an unenforceable anti-miscegenation law was Alabama, which finally repealed its statute banning interracial marriage in 2000.

Despite the South's history of hostility toward interracial marriage, the census bureau found that the southern states, viewed as a region, have the second-highest total of people who reported themselves as "Two or More Races" on their census forms. According to the census bureau, western states have the highest population of people who identified themselves as belonging to "Two or More Races," with 40 percent of the total, while the southern states had 27 percent, northeast states had 18 percent, and the midwest states had 15 percent.

The U.S. military may have a hand in why many people in biracial marriages live in southern states. The military is perhaps the most integrated institution in the United States today. Many military bases are located in the South, so many people who are in the military who choose to get married live in the South. "In the military, everybody's pretty much one color these days," explains Yvette Edgeworth, a black woman whose father made the Air Force his career. Edgeworth, who married a white man and raised three biracial children, met

Some famous biracial Americans include New York Yankees star shortstop Derek Jeter and golf professional Tiger Woods.

her husband while living near Maxwell Air Force Base in Montgomery, Alabama.

In 1960, less than 50,000 marriages were interracial. Today, it is estimated that there are 2 million interracial marriages in the United States, which means that 5 percent of all married people in America are married to someone of a different race. There is a willingness by most young people to consider interracial marriage. According to a Gallup Youth Survey conducted in 2001, 91 percent of the respondents said they could approve of marriages between whites and blacks. In addition, 94 percent of the teenagers who responded to the poll said they could approve of marriages between Hispanic Americans and non-Hispanics, while 93 percent said they could approve of marriages between Asian Americans and non-Asians.

Interracial marriage is an issue the Gallup Organization has

MORE THAN TWO OR MORE RACES

Tiger Woods, arguably the best golfer in the world, describes himself as "Cablinasian"—a mix of Caucasian, black, Native American, and Asian. Woods told talk-show host Oprah Winfrey that he did not want to be considered a person of one particular race. "I'm just who I am, whoever you see in front of you." he said.

The U.S. Census Bureau reported in 2000 that 6.8 million people designated the "Two or More Races" box on their census form, meaning they do not identify themselves as members of a single race. But many people believe, as Tiger Woods does, that they trace their ethnicity to more than two races. The census bureau reported that nearly 500,000 Americans went beyond simply saying they are members of Two or More Races. According to the bureau, 410,285 people said that they are members of three races, 38,408 said they are members of four races, 8,637 said they are members of five races, and 823 people said they belong to six races.

revisited over the years. And each year that the organization studies the issue, it seems the acceptance of interracial marriage among teens rises. In 1977, for example, the Gallup Youth Survey asked teenagers their feelings on marriage between whites and blacks, and just 52 percent said they could approve.

The Gallup Organization did not start asking teens their feelings about interracial marriage involving Hispanics and Asians until 1997; that year, 90 percent of the teens said they could approve of interracial marriage involving Hispanics and non-Hispanics, and 88 percent said they could approve of marriage involving Asians and non-Asians.

Adjusting to Being a Biracial Teen

Adolescence is a difficult time for any young person, whatever their race. It can be a confusing and awkward time for many teens as they undergo changes in their bodies, learn about dating, and experience their first relationships with the opposite sex. Biracial teenagers not only face the pressures of adjusting to adolescence that all teens face, they must also come to terms with their racial identity. Overall, mental health professionals believe biracial teens adjust very well.

A 1992 study at the University of Washington looked at how 44 young people were adjusting to adolescence. Half of the teenagers in the study were biracial, while half were members of a single minority group. The study found that "biracial early adolescents appear to be remarkably similar to other children of color. . . . This does not mean that the adolescents were not experiencing difficulties, either as individuals or as a group. It does imply that to the degree such difficulties were experienced they were no greater in

In addition to adjusting to the pressures faced by all teenagers, biracial teens must also come to terms with their racial identity.

our sample of biracial adolescents than they were in similar adolescents of color."

Of course, biracial teenagers know best how they adopt to the challenges of adolescence. "Now that I'm older, I don't get teased or have any problems with being biracial," Amber W., a 16-year-old Georgia teenager, told a reporter. "But when I was younger, many times I felt like I was white for the black kids and too black for the white kids. I can't win, so I just dealt with it." If she had to choose, Amber said, she would probably identify more with being black, since her skin tone and hair are more similar to her black father's than her white mother's: "I get my hair done at a black hair salon. I use black hair products, date mostly black guys."

Colorado teenager Ian S. told a reporter, "People don't trip on it so much now. It's like everybody is mixed these days." In Detroit, Xiomara B. found hostility at first when she started middle school. Classmates were particularly cruel, writing "Oreo" and other racist names on the bathroom walls. At first, Xiomara ran home in tears. She soon resolved to deal with it. She stood up to her classmates and told them their remarks would not break her spirit. Eventually, the racist comments and jokes died down. "I used to think I wasn't pretty or smart enough, but I woke up one day and realized I was special," she said.

Ann Arbor, Michigan, teenager Stephanie T. said her friends go out of their way to make her feel welcome, but sometimes their attempts are awkward. For example, she said, her black friends feel the need to play the music of white pop stars when she is around. Stephanie thinks that is foolish: "I'm myself, and if they don't like me, that's too bad."

Chapter Five

The growth of the non-English-speaking population in the United States has forced educators to reevaluate systems and strategies in order to accommodate linguistic and cultural barriers to education.

When English Is Not Spoken

Grant Community School in Salem, Oregon, was a school in crisis. During the 1980s and 1990s, the Latino community of Salem had grown mostly through the settlement of thousands of people who migrated to the Pacific Northwest from Latin American countries. They were driven to the region by poverty and civil war at home.

In years past, Hispanic immigrants from Latin American countries tended to settle in large California cities. According to the U.S. Census Bureau, by 1990 foreign-born residents accounted for 20 percent of California's overall population. Californians reacted to the influx of foreign-born people during the 1990s by adopting a number of anti-immigration initiatives, creating a hostile environment for immigrants in the state. As a result, many Latinos moved further north, settling in Oregon and Washington.

That migration placed a strain on public services,

A student at California State University demonstrates against Proposition 209. The referendum question, which was passed by California voters in 1996, abolished programs intended to give Latinos and other minorities greater educational and employment opportunites.

particularly the schools. At Grant Community School, where 40 percent of the students are Latino, the impact soon became obvious. Grant Community School lacked the resources to adequately serve its students, particularly the students who were showing up for classes with very little ability to communicate in English. "This is a high-needs school, designated as such by the school district because lower incomes, higher crime rates, fewer two-parent households, and multicultural diversity characterize its neighborhood," wrote the authors of a 2002 study on bilingual education in the United States. "The school currently serves a population of whom 93.6 percent are from families in poverty."

That report, "A National Study of School Effectiveness for Language Minority Students," was written by researchers at George Mason University in Virginia. The study's authors decided to look at Grant Community School because administrators there realized the depth of their school's problem and did something to turn it around. Grant Community School's solution to the problem was unique—not only did school administrators concentrate on teaching English to Spanish-speaking students, but they elected to put just as much emphasis on teaching Spanish to native-born students as well. "This is a two-way immersion school," explained Principal Grant Foster. "All children who go here learn to read and write in two languages."

Grant Community School's solution was regarded as radical. Starting in 1994, the school recruited bilingual teachers and introduced many Latino-oriented cultural activities into the curriculum. In the classrooms, lessons were taught entirely in English three days a week; for the other two days, lessons were taught entirely in Spanish. This meant that everyone at Grant Community School—not just Latino students—was required to learn a second language. "The real beauty of the program is on the playground," said Foster. "You hear kids speak in English and you hear kids speak in Spanish. . . . The native English speakers help the native Spanish, and on Spanish immersion days the native Spanish speakers help the native English speakers."

Before the school decided to concentrate on elevating all students' communications skills, students at Grant Community School had generally done poorly on scholastic achievement tests. That was particularly true of the Latino students. There is no question the dual-language program helped reverse this trend. "In 2001, the percent of students who met or exceeded the standards of the Oregon Statewide Assessment in grades 3 and 5 was significantly high for this student population," wrote the authors of the George Mason study. "Seventy-four percent of the native English-speaking students met or exceeded the standards in English reading and 58 percent in math. Among the Spanish speakers, 58 percent met or exceeded the standards in English reading and 48 percent in math."

Consequences of a Language Barrier

Grant Community School came up with a groundbreaking way to educate its young people. Most schools do not go to such lengths; in fact, many schools do not offer "English as a Second Language" programs. There is no question, though, that when young foreign-born people are unable to communicate, their opportunities to adjust to U.S. society are severely limited.

"At age 13, Hispanic students were, on average, about two years behind in math and reading, and about four years behind in science," said the U.S. Department of Education in a 1996 report

on scholastic achievement by Latinos. "In fact, 40 percent of 16- to 24-year-old Hispanic dropouts left school with less than a 9th grade education, compared with 13 percent of white dropouts and 11 percent of black dropouts." The report continued:

> Once a student falls behind, the effects may last a lifetime. Rather than face continuous humiliation, many Latino students simply walk away from formal education. It is essential to understand that each step in the educational system is a building block. When steps are missed, the results often lead to poor performance, grade retention, and dropping out. Large gaps in educational attainment remain through the age of 17, with Latino students scoring lower than white students in math, science, reading and writing proficiency.

The U.S. Department of Education said that in 1993, 28 percent of all Latinos had dropped out of high school—double the rate for blacks and nearly three times the rate for whites. Also, the agency found that Latinos not only drop out in higher numbers than blacks and whites, but they drop out of school earlier than

Newcomers to the United States for whom English is a second language lag behind native-born Americans in education and therefore in opportunities for their future. A young person who drops out of school early is more likely to work at a low-income job with few benefits or opportunities for growth. Unfortunately, the dropout rate for Latinos is much higher than for members of other racial groups.

other young people. "In 1993, an alarming 40 percent of Hispanic dropouts had not completed the 8th grade," said the department of education report. "Another 18 percent of Latino dropouts completed the 9th grade but left before completing the 10th grade and

CONVINCING LATINOS TO GO TO COLLEGE

In 2002, the Bush administration announced an initiative to convince more Latinos to attend college. According to the U.S. Education Department, just 6 percent of all associate degrees were awarded to Latinos in 1992. In addition, the agency reported, Latinos received just 4 percent of bachelor's degrees, 3 percent of master's degrees, and 2 percent of doctorates awarded in 1992.

"Actual numbers of PhD's awarded demonstrate the magnitude of the degree disparities," said a report by the department. "In 1994, of the 43,261 PhD's awarded across all fields in U.S. colleges and universities, only 946 were awarded to Hispanics, while 11,530 were awarded to foreign national or alien students, 1,344 to black students, 132 to American Indians or Alaskan Natives, 1,943 to Asian Americans, and 26,137 to white students. There are entire fields of disciplines at the doctoral level in which Hispanics and other minorities have never received a doctoral degree."

The Tomas Rivera Policy Institute, a California-based organization that studies Hispanic American issues, found that few Latino parents understand what it takes to get a student ready for a college education or to make financial plans to make college a reality for their sons and daughters.

The Bush administration believes that Latinos should be preparing for college educations. To help students and parents understand the challenges they must overcome to make college a reality, the administration established a bilingual World Wide Web site that contains information on college costs as well as questions about academic goals that students should be raising with themselves and their college guidance counselors. The Internet address for the page is www.YesICan.gov. Visitors to the Web site can find the character "Pablo the Eagle," whose job is to encourage reading by young Hispanic children. The Hispanic Broadcasting Corporation, which provides Latino programming to 55 radio stations in the United States, promised to broadcast public service announcements promoting the Web site to its listeners.

over one-half—58 percent—of Hispanic dropouts have less than a 10th grade education. Only 29 percent of white dropouts and 25 percent of black dropouts leave as early as do Hispanics."

Problems Faced by Immigrants

The U.S. Census Bureau says that one in ten people who live in the United States were born in another country—the highest percentage of foreign-born Americans since 1930. Many of these foreign-born people are coming to the United States from Latin America; in 1997, according to the U.S. Census Bureau, 13.1 million people—or about one in two foreign-born residents—were from Latin American countries.

There are many statistics that show that Latinos are at a disadvantage in the United States. Young people from Latin America lag behind native-born people in obtaining higher education. The U.S. Census Bureau reports that only 47 percent of Latin American-born people who live in the United States seek some form of higher education after high school. In comparison, 84 percent of native-born Americans go on to study at a college or trade school. Of course, if fewer Latinos are seeking higher education, fewer Latinos can expect to obtain quality jobs. Thirty percent of native-born Americans hold professional or management jobs; just 11 percent of Latinos born outside the United States hold professional or managerial jobs.

Lower-quality jobs usually come with low pay. The census bureau reported that the median income for a household of Latinos born outside the United States is $24,100 a year. Median income for a household of native-born Americans is $36,100 a year. A lower-quality job usually means inadequate health benefits as well. In the United States, most people rely on their employers to pay a large portion of their health insurance costs, but companies that offer employment for menial labor typically offer no health insurance benefits. According to the U.S. Census Bureau, 54 percent of native-born Americans have health insurance coverage, while just 36 percent of Latinos born outside the United States are covered by health insurance plans.

Sixty-eight percent of native-born American families own their own homes; just 38 percent of Latino families born outside the United States are homeowners. There are more Latinos living in poverty. The Census Bureau reported that 28 percent of people in the United States who were born in Latin America are living in poverty; just 13 percent of the native-born U.S. population lives in impoverished circumstances.

At the root of many of the problems faced by young Latinos is their inability to speak English and understand instructions or advice when they are written in English. Many young Latinos come from homes in which their parents do not speak English. In 1999, the U.S. Department of Education reported that 43 percent of Hispanic students in U.S. schools went home each afternoon to households where English was not spoken. In 2000, the department reported, "Hispanic students who were enrolled in grades kindergarten through 5 were more likely than those enrolled in the higher grades to speak mostly Spanish at home." Things do not improve much as the child grows older. The U.S. Department of Education reported that 37 percent of students in the sixth through eighth grades live in homes where Spanish is the only language spoken, while 38 percent of students in the ninth through twelfth grades go home to parents who do not speak English.

To say that schools have not responded to the needs of Latino students would be wrong. Although few schools have responded in the way Grant Community School attacked its problem, many school districts with Hispanic populations have introduced some form of education for students who speak English as a second language. The U.S. Department of Education reports that more than 3.4 million students are enrolled in so-called Limited-English Proficient Programs. However, the U.S. Census Bureau reports

These Spanish-speaking students in a Texas elementary school are part of a dual-language program. Sixty percent of the school's student population is Hispanic, so kindergarten and first-grade students spend half of their school day studying reading, writing, and arithmetic in Spanish, and the second half of the day learning the lessons in English. Educators believe that programs like this will help close the "achievement gap" between non-English speaking students and native English speakers.

that in 2000, there were 8.6 million Hispanics between the ages of 5 and 18 living in the United States. Although not all of those young people require Limited-English Proficient Programs, it is obvious that many young Latinos are not receiving the English-language education they need.

Local politics has a lot to do with why some communities are hostile toward meeting the needs of Latino students. Politicians who are under pressure to balance their governments' budgets and keep taxes low may be unwilling to spend the money it takes to provide education in English to Latinos, who are certainly underrepresented in Congress and state legislatures and, there-fore, have little political power. According to the Department of Education:

> The issue is not whether it is more expensive to educate Hispanic Americans, the issue is that the districts where Hispanic children reside are usually low-wealth districts that generate less funding from property taxes. Also, most Hispanic Americans live in urban areas. Urban schools are older and often have dilapidated buildings. In most cases, districts have to pass bond referendums to build schools, which are often not supported by the general voting public. Therefore, school districts with concentrations of Hispanic American students remain under-funded and must seek other means of support.

As for whether school districts would also be willing to pay for Limited-English Proficient Programs, the U.S. Department of Education report said, "One of the most controversial issues in the education of Hispanic children is language. The reason for this controversy is primarily political, rather than educational, and reflect a public misunderstanding that bilingual and English-as-a-Second-Language education methods are somehow a threat to American culture and values."

The Gallup Youth Survey has looked at language programs in schools. In 1997, 60 percent of teenagers who participated in a

Gallup Youth Survey poll said Limited-English Proficient Programs should be made available in the schools. Sixty-four percent of the respondents said that they attended school with students for whom English is a second language.

Of course, Latinos are not the only immigrants who find themselves overcoming language barriers. Following the break-up of the Soviet Union, many Russians and Eastern Europeans found the opportunity to immigrate to the United States. People from China, Vietnam, and other countries of Asia have found a haven in the United States as well. The Census Bureau reported that of the 26 million foreign-born people living in the United States in 1997, 6.8 million came from Asia and 4.3 million from Europe. All of them find that to adjust to life in the United States, they must learn to speak and understand English.

The English-only Movement

Not everyone supports the use of more than one language in the United States. In the spring of 2003, voters in Reading, Pennsylvania, were for the first time given the opportunity to cast their ballots on voting machines in which the candidates' names, offices, and instructions for voting were printed in Spanish. (An estimated 37 percent of the population of Reading is Hispanic.) The ballots were printed in Spanish after the U.S. Justice Department sued elections officials of Berks County, where Reading is located, alleging that the county government violated the U.S. Voting Rights Act by engaging in "hostile and unequal" treatment of Latino voters—excluding bilingual ballots at most polling places and resorting to other tactics to deny Latino voters access to the polls. "There are several issues that were in play," said Jorge Martinez, a spokesman for the Justice Department.

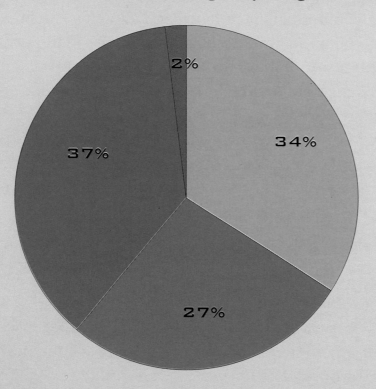

THE LANGUAGE OF EDUCATION

Which of the following three approaches is the best way for public schools to deal with non-English speaking students?

2%

34%

37%

27%

- Put the students in classes taught in English with minimum tutoring needed to help them learn English.

- Provide public school instruction in all subjects in the students' native language while they learn English.

- Require students to learn English in public schools before they receive instruction in any other subjects.

- Don't know/refused to answer.

Poll taken June 1998; 4,341 total respondents.
Source: The Gallup Organization

"One was poll workers denying a person's right to vote, being overtly hostile to Latino voters, specifically Puerto Ricans. Finally, they were asking for more identification than they asked [for from] white voters." A federal judge ruled in favor of the Justice Department, forcing the Berks County Board of Elections to make bilingual ballots available to all voters. On Election Day, court-appointed observers were dispatched to Reading to make sure the judge's orders were obeyed.

What happened in Reading is not unusual. Across the United States, Latinos and others who lack English skills have often been denied their rights. There has long been an "English Only" movement, which aims to declare English the official language of the United States. People who support the movement believe that street signs, subway platform signs, tax forms, drivers' license examinations, election ballots, and thousands of other communications published by the government should be in one language—English.

Although English is spoken by nearly everyone who lives in the United States, the U.S. Constitution does not designate an official language. According to the U.S. Census Bureau, Americans speak more than 300 languages. Twenty-three states have adopted English as their official language; the most recent was Iowa in 2002. The depth of the laws and the verve in which they are enforced differ from state to state. Iowa, for example, requires that most government documents be printed in English, but makes exceptions for driver's education materials, trade and tourism publications, and documents dealing with the rights of victims of crimes, criminal defendants, and constitutional issues. California declared English the official state language in 1986, and yet each year Los Angeles City Council spends $1 million to publish its legal advertisements in six different languages. Arizona passed an English-only law in 1988 that was so restrictive it was declared unconstitutional in 1996 by the state supreme court, which found it violated the right to free speech of people who lack English language skills.

One issue that angers English-only advocates is bilingual education in schools. They do not oppose Limited-English Proficient Programs, in which foreign-born students learn to communicate in English. Instead, they oppose programs in which both English and Spanish are used for teaching. "Parents know that the English language is the most important thing their child needs to learn in school," insists Mauro E. Mujica, chairman of U.S. English, an organization dedicated to establishing English as the country's official language. "By blocking reform of bilingual education, the educational establishment is denying many children the key to future success: as the foreman on a ranch in Texas so eloquently put it, 'My children learn Spanish in school so they can grow up to be busboys and waiters. I teach them English at home so they can grow up to be doctors and lawyers.'"

The ACLU disagrees. The public interest lobby has long opposed the English-only movement, and has helped overturn English-only laws in several states. The ACLU's view on the issue is explained in the following statement:

> The primary purpose of bilingual programs in elementary and secondary schools, which use both English and a child's native language to teach all subjects, is to develop proficiency in English and, thus, to facilitate the child's transition to all-English instruction. . . . The latest studies show that bilingual education definitely enhances a child's ability to acquire the second language. Some studies even show that the more extensive the native language instruction, the better students perform all around, and that the bilingual method engenders a positive self-image and self-respect by validating the child's native language and culture.

The evidence seems to support the ACLU's position. After all, the achievement scores at Grant Community School rose after administrators stepped up their efforts to provide bilingual education. In the past, the ACLU said, children of immigrants were forced to "sink or swim" by sitting in classrooms in which all the instruction was in English. That experience, the ACLU said, "left more of them underwater than not."

Chapter Six

John Sie, chairman of an entertainment company, announces the launch of new television public service announcements intended to discourage ethnic stereotyping of Muslim Americans. After Muslim extremists carried out deadly terrorist attacks against targets in the U.S. on September 11, 2001, some Arab Americans and Muslims in the United States became the target of retaliatory attacks.

Young Muslims in America

The United States acted swiftly and decisively following the September 11, 2001, terrorist attacks on the World Trade Center in New York and the Pentagon outside Washington, D.C. The U.S. military was quickly sent to Afghanistan, where it rooted out members of the al-Qaeda terrorist network and overthrew the fundamentalist Taliban government that had been shielding them.

While much of the nation's hostility following the September 11 attacks was aimed at al-Qaeda and the Taliban, a measure of hate was also directed toward innocent Muslims living in the United States. The incidents chronicled in the press included:

In Illinois, hundreds of youths staged anti-Islamic demonstrations in the streets for several nights after the September 11 attacks.

* * *

On the day after the attack, a gas station in Indiana owned by a Yemeni immigrant was bombarded with gunfire.

* * *

In Anaheim, three teenagers smashed the windows of Sinbad Ranch Market, a business owned by Arab immigrants.

* * *

In Texas, bottles of liquor and homemade bombs were tossed at an Islamic school.

* * *

In San Francisco, an Islamic leader cautioned Muslim women to protect themselves by not venturing out of their homes.

In the fall of 2001, such incidents were not uncommon in the United States, even though President George W. Bush admonished people to remember that Muslim Americans were not the enemy. "No one should be singled out for unfair treatment or unkind words because of their ethnic background or religious faith," the president told the nation. Still, the incidents continued and Muslim teenagers did not escape the backlash. "My mom's friends are scared to step out of the house and drive their kids to school because they don't know what people are going to do," said Hoda A., a Muslim student who attended high school in Florida. "This is the first time I've had to deal with something this major. . . . I've been strong enough to handle this myself. I'm not afraid."

Renee H., a Muslim-American teenager from Connecticut, told a reporter that many of the people he knew in high school stopped being his friend. Now, Renee said, he is afraid to tell people that he is a Muslim: "I am afraid of people's prejudice and their allegations."

The Growth of the Muslim Population

Muslim Americans are believed to be one of the fastest growing ethnic groups in the United States. Nevertheless, it is difficult to tell how many Muslims live in America. The U.S. Census Bureau is prohibited from asking people their religious affiliations.

Other governmental agencies, as well as private institutions, have made estimates, however. The U.S. State Department estimates that there are about 6 million Muslims living in the United States. Of this number, it is estimated that about 23 percent, or 1.4 million Muslims, are under the age of 18. Muslims currently are the third-largest religious group in the country, after Christians and Jews; after 2010 it is estimated that Muslims will pass Jews to become the second-largest group.

The State Department estimates that about 25 percent of Muslims immigrated to the United States from the Middle East, while another 25 percent came from countries in south Asia. About 15 percent of the Muslim population immigrated to the

Rescue workers drape a large American flag over the side of the damaged Pentagon building. In the weeks after the September 11, 2001, terrorist attacks, patriotic feelings in the United States reached high levels; tragically, in some people those feelings escalated into violence toward Muslims and others who looked "different."

U.S. from other countries, the state department reports, while about 35 percent are native born. Of those who are native born, the majority are black.

Many Middle Eastern immigrants are not Muslim. A study of religious affiliation conducted by the City University of New York found that there are some 3.5 million Americans who have Arabic heritage, yet just twenty-five percent of them are Muslims. The remaining 75 percent are mostly Christians, including a large population of Lebanese, Iraqis, Egyptians, and Syrians who came to the United States to escape religious persecution in their home countries. Many non-Muslims from Iran, which is not an Arabic country, have immigrated to the United States. "Put simply," the City University study said, "the majority of Arab Americans are not Muslims and the majority of Muslims are not Arab Americans."

Muslim American Life in the United States

Muslim Americans have tried to settle into lives in the United States while retaining important aspects of their religion and culture. The Sabr Foundation, which promotes Islamic education and culture, estimates that there are more than 800 mosques in the United States, as well as 165 private Islamic religious schools. According to the foundation, there are more than 400 associations of Muslim Americans and nearly 100 newspapers, magazines, and other publications published for Muslim readers.

Although degrees of religious observance varies among Muslims, just as it does among followers of other faiths, most Muslim American observe the most important Islamic laws. Many Muslim women keep their heads covered, and most Muslims also observe their religion's strict dietary laws, and the restrictions on alcohol, tobacco, and drugs. Muslims also observe Ramadan, a month of fasting and self-sacrifice during which they are encouraged to devote more time to meditation, strengthening their relationships with friends and family members, and studying the Qur'an.

For young Muslims trying to fit into American society, observing Ramadan has its challenges. For example, during Ramadan Muslims are not permitted to eat or drink during the day. Without food, Muslim student athletes may find themselves growing weary as they train or compete in rigorous sporting events. "You get tired," explains Abdullah B., a football player at a Michigan high school. "You get tired real fast." During Ramadan, Abdullah would practice all week on an empty stomach, even refusing to sip water between plays. At Fordson High School in Michigan, 61 of the 65 players on the football team are Muslim. Before and

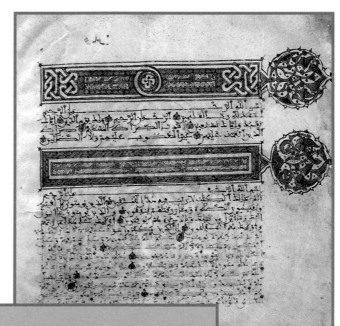

An ornate illustrated page from the Qur'an, the holy scriptures of Islam. The Qur'an provides guidance on how Muslims are supposed to live their daily lives.

Muslim worshippers pray during the service at the Masjid Al-Abidin mosque in New York. Muslims are the third-largest religious group in the United States, with a population estimated at 6 million. There are about 1.25 billion Muslims worldwide.

after every game, and at each halftime, the players gather on the field to recite Muslim prayers. The coach, Jeff Sterglas, told a reporter he admires his students' dedication. "As a non-Muslim, I respect the discipline they have to do it," he said. "And by doing this, it makes them a better person."

Elsewhere, young Muslim Americans find other ways to maintain their culture while remaining a part of American society. On college campuses, for example, many Muslim American students try not to take classes on Friday afternoons, which is reserved for a traditional congregational prayer. Some colleges have responded to the needs of their Muslim students by hiring part-time religious leaders to lead Muslim prayer services and by setting aside facilities on the campuses to serve as mosques. "It's not coming at odds with the rest of the campus," says Altaf Husain, national president of the 500-chapter Muslim Students Association. "It's almost like saying while everyone else has their rights we would like to have our rights."

On many campuses, young Muslims and Jews find it hard to get along. In the Middle East, Muslims and Jews have clashed since the state of Israel was established in 1948. Over the years, the Islamic nations and Israel have engaged in armed conflict. In recent years, as plans to establish a homeland for Palestinian Arabs in the Israeli-occupied West Bank territory have stalled, Palestinian terrorist groups have sponsored suicide bombing missions that have killed hundreds of Israelis. For American Muslims and Jews, it is often hard for them to encounter one another on campus without thinking of the hostile climate in the Middle East.

Additionally, many young Muslims find their loyalties as American citizens divided. As the U.S. responded to the terrorist attacks of September 11 by invading Afghanistan, and later as U.S. military forces prepared for war against Iraq, Muslim students could not help but wonder how Islamic people had become enemies of the United States. Some young Muslims said they had a hard time justifying warfare on Muslim citizens of other countries under any circumstances. Many are openly hostile toward U.S. wars against Islamic nations like Afghanistan and Iraq. They insist that if called on to fight for the United States against a Muslim state, they would refuse to serve.

The Attitudes of Young People

The Gallup Youth Survey has examined the impact of terrorism on young people several times since the September 11, 2001, attacks on the Pentagon and World Trade Center. In April 2003, the Gallup Youth Survey asked 1,200 teenagers between the ages of 13 and 17 to name the most important problem facing people their age. Sixteen percent cited drug abuse, down from 41 percent in a

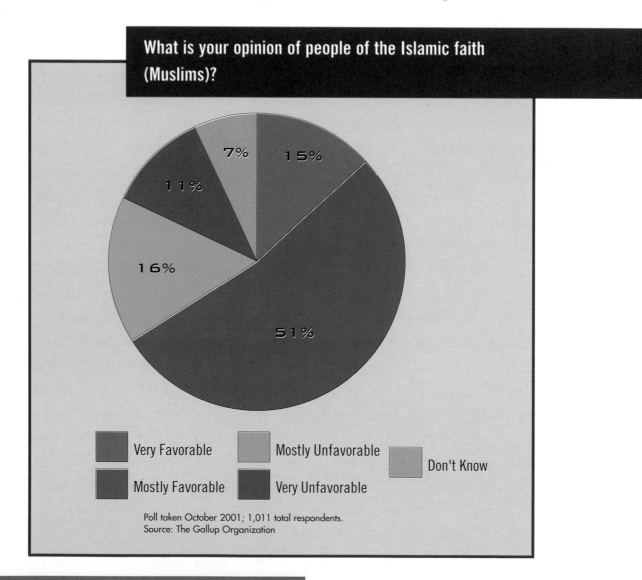

What is your opinion of people of the Islamic faith (Muslims)?

- 15%
- 7%
- 11%
- 16%
- 51%

Very Favorable — Mostly Unfavorable — Don't Know

Mostly Favorable — Very Unfavorable

Poll taken October 2001; 1,011 total respondents.
Source: The Gallup Organization

1997 poll. Terrorism, which had not been included in the 1997 poll, was cited by 12 percent of the young people who responded.

A similar poll conducted in March 2003 asked 1,200 teenagers between the ages of 13 and 17 to rate factors or events that are likely to impact their futures. "Political terrorists" was rated near the top of the list of factors, with 89 percent of respondents believing terrorism would have an impact on their futures. Seventy-one percent of the respondents feared that "religious fanatics" would also have an impact on their futures.

In May 2003, after President George W. Bush announced an end to major combat in Iraq, the Gallup Youth Survey published the results of a poll in which 1,200 teenagers were asked whether racial, religious, or lifestyle practices would affect their choices of college roommates. On the question of religious differences, Muslims ranked high on the list of roommates whom teens said they would prefer to avoid. According to the poll, 29 percent of the respondents said they would rather not share their college dormitory rooms with people of the Islamic faith. (Thirty-seven percent of the respondents said they would have the most difficulty accepting a roommate who was an atheist, while 27 percent of teens indicated they did not wish to room with members of the religious right.)

Overall, though, 63 percent of the respondents said it "makes no difference" to them if they were asked to room with a Muslim student. Still, given the number of young people who indicate they would rather not share a dorm room with a Muslim, it appears that young Muslims will continue to bear the unfortunate burden of mistrust and suspicion that was heaped upon them following the acts of terrorism committed on September 11, 2001.

Chapter Seven

Even though minority teens living in urban areas or distressed neighbor-hoods often receive educations that are inferior to those of affluent suburban students, many are able to continue on to college thanks to "affirmative action" programs. However, the constitutionality of these programs is under attack by various groups.

Each Student Is an Individual

Michelle D. grew up in an inner-city neighborhood in Philadelphia. After graduating from high school, the African-American student looked back and realized the education she received at one of the city's distressed schools had not prepared her for college. "My experience in high school was absolutely unfair," Michelle told a reporter in 2003. "We never were assigned to write an essay. We never really read books. The standard of education was so low. How do you expect that preparation would put us on an equal footing with students who went to white, privileged high schools? Isn't that discrimination?"

Despite those disadvantages, Michelle was still regarded as college material by Ursinus College, a private institution in the Philadelphia suburbs. She graduated from Ursinus in 2003 and was accepted as a graduate student that year at George Washington University in Washington, D.C.

She was able to accomplish all that because even though her high school could not measure up to most schools attended by whites, Ursinus College still believed she had the intelligence and talent to succeed. And so Ursinus accepted Michelle as a student, made financial aid available to her so she could afford the tuition, and even provided Michelle with a summertime orientation program designed specifically to assist minority students.

Nevertheless, as Michelle prepared to graduate from Ursinus, two cases reached the U.S. Supreme Court that alleged what colleges had done for her and for other minority students was unfair to white students. Those cases charged that colleges had gone too far in their affirmative action goals, making it too easy for minority students to obtain entry into schools that used a second and much more difficult standard when considering white people for admission and scholarships.

A Brief History of Affirmative Action

The term *affirmative action* was first used in 1961, when President John F. Kennedy created the Equal Employment Opportunity Commission (EEOC). The president told contractors working on government projects to "take affirmative action to ensure that applicants are employed without regard to race, creed, color, or national origin."

Three years later, President Lyndon B. Johnson signed the Civil Rights Act of 1964, which banned racial discrimination in the workplace. In 1965, Johnson signed Executive Order 11246, which directed contractors seeking work from the federal government to ensure that they extended employment opportunities to members of historically disadvantaged groups—women, African

Americans, Hispanics, Native Americans, Asians, and Pacific Islanders. Johnson's intent was to increase opportunities for women and minorities, but his executive order did not provide much specific guidance. Still, given the history and extent of discrimination it was clear that definitive steps had to be taken for Johnson's goals to be met.

Affirmative action was not confined to the workplace. During the 1960s, most college students were affluent whites. This indicated that many minorities were being frozen out of higher education. Some college administrators began to question what kind of educations they were providing if most of their students came from similar backgrounds. The only people those students would meet during their college careers would be other affluent whites. "Racial, ethnic and gender diversity in collegiate settings helps to stimulate students' personal growth and intellectual development," said a report published by the American Psychological Association. The organization's report adds:

> Exposure to the educational environment during late adolescence and early adulthood is important for enabling critical thinking, fostering participation in civil life and intellectual development that is deeper and involves more active mental alertness and problem solving. The opportunity for minority and nonminority students to interact with each other may foster this kind of intellectual development by exposing the students to alternative perspectives and cultural frameworks and by challenging students' assumptions.

In 1955, a year after the *Brown v. Board of Education* decision, fewer than 5 percent of American college students were black. By 1990, that number had grown to 11 percent—a number that was closer to being representative of the overall percentage of African Americans in the United States. In the years between 1955 and 1990, colleges had taken steps toward diversifying their student bodies. In many cases, colleges were urged to diversify by the U.S.

When President Lyndon B. Johnson issued Executive Order 11246 in September 1965, it provided for fair, nondiscriminatory employment practices. The scope of the order was soon expanded to cover public education, and many institutions of higher learning began efforts to diversify their student populations.

Department of Education and other federal agencies. By the 1980s, colleges found themselves questioned by the department of education on which high schools their recruiters were visiting and on how they were selling themselves to minorities in their promotional literature.

But the methods that colleges had used to become diversified were also being challenged during this time. During the 1970s, a white student named Alan Bakke, who wanted to study medicine, sued the University of California at Davis. Bakke claimed that the university had discriminated against him, by rejecting his application for admission twice while at the same time accepting minority students with weaker academic records and lower test scores.

The University of California admitted 100 students a year to the medical school at its Davis campus. Sixteen of those 100 places were reserved for minority students. Bakke had first applied for admission in 1973 and was rejected. After the university rejected his application again in 1974, Bakke filed a lawsuit in federal court, arguing that he had been turned down for admission solely because of race. Bakke alleged in his suit that the university violated his rights under the Civil Rights Act of 1964 — the law that was intended to provide equal opportunity to all Americans.

In 1978 the U.S. Supreme Court ruled in the Bakke case that the university's affirmative action plan had violated the U.S. Constitution's guarantee of equal protection under the law. The court found that Bakke had been denied admission to the university's medical school for no reason other than race. The court's decision cleared the way for Bakke to enter the medical school; He went on to graduate and pursue a successful career as a doctor.

Alan Bakke (center) is surrounded by reporters and photographers while leaving class after his first day at the University of California at Davis Medical School, September 1978. Bakke won a historic "reverse discrimination" suit in which the Supreme Court set guidelines for school affirmative action policies.

Although the Supreme Court struck down the University of California at Davis' affirmative action plan, the Court did not eliminate the concept of affirmative action. Instead, the court simply found that a quota system—in which a certain number of places are reserved for members of a particular group—was unconstitutional. Universities were still free to pursue diversity in their student bodies. They were even permitted to take race into consideration as one of a number of factors in the admission process, as long as this was done on a case-by-case basis. Nevertheless, schools were specifically prohibited from designating a set number of places in their classrooms for minority students. Quotas, the court ruled, were illegal.

After Bakke

Over the next several years, colleges continued to recruit minorities. African Americans, Latinos, and others were offered financial aid as well as entry into special programs to help them assimilate to life on campus. At Ursinus, for example, Michelle D. participated in the school's "Bridge" program, which was set up to aid first-year minority students. While attending Ursinus as a freshman, Michelle recalled spending some time with other minority students in the nearby town of Collegeville, which has a predominantly white population, and hearing a racial epithet shouted at them. "If it was just me, I'd have been scared and wanted to go home," she said. But Michelle said the students in the Bridge program were able to confront the issue of racism, talk it over, and deal with it.

Nevertheless, by the 1990s affirmative action on college campuses was again under siege. Critics wondered whether schools, while not using quotas, were taking other steps to enhance minority enrollment at the expense of qualified whites. And they also wondered whether affirmative action had truly been successful. Certainly, there was no questioning the numbers—more minority students were enrolled in the nation's colleges than ever before. But were the minority students really being assimilated? Did white students and black students learn from one another? To many critics, it seemed as though they were not. They pointed out that once on campus, black students tended to room together, eat together, and socialize mostly with one another; white students continued to live their lives apart from the other races as well. Critics contended that the minority-only prep sessions held before commencement of regular classes seemed only to help minority students bond with one another rather than help them bond with whites. "That's a fair criticism," said Nancy Vickers, president of Bryn Mawr College, a Pennsylvania school that invites minority students onto campus a week before regular fall classes begin. "But minorities say the program is among the single most important experiences of college. We need to strike a balance between the comfort zone for students of different backgrounds wanting to find people like themselves and what we can achieve socially by bringing minority groups on campus."

Some students argue that they would never have the opportunity to meet minority students unless their colleges actively recruit them. "My freshman dorm was like the United Nations," said Swarthmore College student Jacquelene K. "My roommate was from Singapore. Down the hall was someone from Ireland. Upstairs was someone from Nigeria."

In 1997, Jennifer Gratz and Patrick Hamacher, two students who had been turned down for admission to the University of Michigan, filed suit against the school, contending that their

A University of Michigan student demonstrates in support of the school's affirmative action program in 1998. In June 2003, the U.S. Supreme Court ruled that the university's undergraduate affirmative action policy, which awarded points to students based on their race, was unconstitutional.

rejections had been based solely on race. In their case, the two plaintiffs alleged that the university's College of Literature, Science, and Arts maintained a point system when assessing potential students. Under the point system, a potential student needed at least 100 out of a maximum of 150 points to be admitted. However, attorneys for Gratz and Hamacher alleged, the university automatically gave African Americans, Latinos, and other minority students 20 points based on their race or ethnic backgrounds.

A separate case against the University of Michigan was also filed that year. In that case, Barbara Grutter, a 48-year-old Michigan woman, initiated a lawsuit alleging that she had been denied admission to the university's law school on the basis of race. In the Grutter case, attorneys did not cite a point system or some other method of specifically giving an advantage to a prospective minority student. Instead, her attorneys called into question the whole concept of affirmative action in an attempt to overturn the Supreme Court's decision in the Bakke case.

As the two cases made their way slowly through the courts, the country found itself divided on the issue. Several groups that champion conservative causes joined the case, underwriting the legal costs incurred in the effort to end affirmative action. In Washington, D.C., the Republican administration of President George W. Bush sided with plaintiffs, asking the courts to overturn the Bakke decision. In early 2003, the Supreme Court announced it would hear arguments on the Grutter and Gratz-Hamacher cases.

"This is a big issue that the Supreme Court needs to decide," said Kirk Kolbo, an attorney for Grutter. "The University of Michigan cases have extensive factual records showing that the [university] employs a heavy hand in the use of race in admissions." University officials insisted, though, that affirmative action has a place in the admissions process. University of Michigan President Mary Sue Coleman said, "This is a historic opportunity for the court to reaffirm Bakke so that all institutions of higher education will have the academic freedom to take race into account."

As the war of words continued, Americans found themselves deeply divided over the future of affirmative action. A 2003 study by Marist College in Poughkeepsie, New York, found that most people thought diversity on college campuses benefited students, but most people also opposed the consideration of race in admissions. "The American public is somewhat conflicted on this issue," said Marist College President Dennis Murray. "Even minority groups feel that race alone should not be a deciding factor in who is admitted and who is not."

A Gallup Youth Survey conducted in 2003 found that young people were also divided on the issue. The Gallup Organization surveyed a total of 1,200 teens between the ages of 13 and 17. Fifty-five percent favored affirmative action programs on college campuses; 44 percent said they opposed them. In addition, the Gallup Youth Survey found that teens who are members of minority groups are much more supportive of affirmative action than white teens. That poll found that 76 percent of nonwhite teens favor affirmative action, while just 45 percent of white teens thought race should be considered during the college admission process.

Meanwhile, changes began occurring on college campuses—some of them prompted by the courts, some by state governments, and some by the colleges themselves. For example, at the University of Michigan the school dropped its point system even before the Supreme Court ruled on its constitutionality.

The University of Michigan is not the only school that had to revise its affirmative action policy in recent years. At the University of Texas, a similar system had been established to recruit minority students—a fact that came to light after a student named Cheryl Hopwood sued the school. In 1992, Hopwood was rejected by the law school of the University of Texas, even though she had earned a grade point average of 3.8 out of a possible 4.0 and scored in the 83rd percentile on the Law School Admissions Test. Hopwood sued, alleging reverse discrimination. Soon, her lawyers discovered that the school used a two-track admissions process. Applications were color-coded by race—white, Asian, and some Hispanic students went through a screening process with one set of standards; African American and Mexican American applicants were considered by a separate panel that used more lenient rules. Hopwood's lawyers argued that her grade-point average and test scores gave her a point total that was higher than all but one of the approximately 25 black students who were enrolled at the school and all but three of the 50 Mexican American students who had been admitted. During the trial, the law school admitted that its two-track policy was illegal. In 1996, a federal appeals court determined that the affirmative action policy at the law school of the University of Texas was unconstitutional.

A result was that the population of minority students fell dramatically. Within a year of the court's ruling in the Hopwood case, Latino enrollment at the University of Texas law school dropped by 64 percent; black enrollment dropped by 88 percent.

In 1996, a year after the Hopwood decision, California voters passed a referendum known as Proposition 209, which barred any consideration of race or ethnic background in the state university system, which is the largest in the nation. Minority enrollment at the state universities quickly fell. At the University of California campus at Berkeley, minority enrollment dropped by half. Law school admissions throughout California's state university system saw a 72 percent decrease in black students and a 35 percent decrease in Latino students. Florida followed California's lead; in 1999 Florida Governor Jeb Bush issued Executive Order 99-281, ending affirmative action in state contracting and university admissions.

Legislatures in Florida and Texas attempted to compensate for the loss of affirmative action programs in their states by passing laws guaranteeing state university admissions to top students. In

Florida, for example, students who graduate in the top 20 percent of their high-school graduating classes are guaranteed admission to state universities, while in Texas admission is guaranteed to students who finish in the top 10 percent of their classes. Legislators hoped these measures would help level the playing field for minority students who attend distressed high schools. Even though the educations that students receive at those schools may be of lesser quality than the educations that students in more affluent areas could expect at their schools, students who work hard and do well in relation to other students at their schools are guaranteed an opportunity for higher education.

Elsewhere, conservative groups convinced a number of colleges to revamp minority-only scholarship programs as well as their prep sessions for freshmen, threatening legal action if they continued to offer them only to minorities. "We're not out to kill these programs," said Edward Blum, director of legal affairs for the American Civil Rights Institute. "Most sound like great programs. But any kids from disadvantaged economic backgrounds could make good use of these." Added Roger Clegg, vice president for the Center for Equal Opportunity: "Schools shouldn't be sorting students by skin color. They're creating and encouraging students to segregate."

Against this most divisive backdrop of emotions and uncertainty about the future course of affirmative action, in 2003 the U.S. Supreme Court issued its rulings in the Gratz-Hamacher and Grutter cases. In Gratz-Hamacher, the nine members of the Supreme Court voted 6–3 to overturn the University of Michigan's point system, finding it unconstitutional. That decision was not a surprise—even the university had conceded as much when it dropped the point system on its own.

In the Court's opinion in the Gratz-Hamacher case, Chief Justice William Rehnquist wrote that the Court in the Bakke decision held that "each characteristic of a particular applicant was to be considered in assessing the applicant's entire application." Under Bakke, he said, one of those characteristics could be race. Clearly, Rehnquist said, a standardized system of awarding points based on race went beyond individualized consideration. "We find that the university's policy, which automatically distributes 20 points, or one-fifth of the points needed to guarantee admission, to every single 'underrepresented minority' applicant solely because of race, is not narrowly tailored to achieve the interest in

Students at the University of California, Berkeley, protest California's ban on affirmative action programs. After Proposition 209 was passed in 1996, enrollment of African American, Hispanic, and Native American students in the state university system dropped dramatically. By 2000, 75 percent of the incoming freshmen at Berkeley were white or Asian; 9 percent of the incoming freshman population was Hispanic, while just 4 percent was African American.

Do you favor or oppose affirmative action programs for minorities and women for admission to colleges and universities?

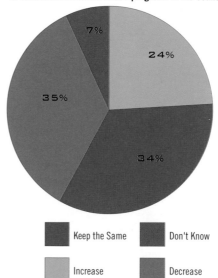

Favor   Oppose   Don't know

Do you think affirmative action has been good for the country, or do you think it has not been good?

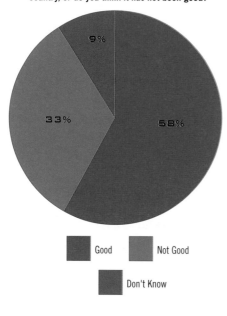

Good   Not Good

Don't Know

In general, do you think we need to increase, keep the same, or decrease affirmative action programs in the country?

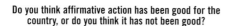

Keep the Same   Don't Know

Increase   Decrease

Poll taken August 2001; 1,017 total respondents.
Source: The Gallup Organization

educational diversity that [the university] claims justifies their program," wrote Rehnquist.

In the Grutter case, the Supreme Court ruled 5–4 that affirmative action could still be used in the college admissions process as long as schools continued to abide by the rules established in the Bakke decision: no point systems, no quotas, no color-coding of applications, no computerized formulas that would add weight to applications based on students' racial and ethnic backgrounds, or any other institutionalized system to make sure minority students have an edge over white students. In fact, the Supreme Court ruled, colleges must assess each student as an individual, even if that process proved to be long and painstaking. For example, Justice Sandra Day O'Connor wrote that just because a student earned low test scores or did poorly in high school did not necessarily mean the student should automatically be excluded from admission to the school; instead, the college could consider other variables—such as community service, recommendations from teachers, and the impact of the student's race on the school's efforts to diversify its campus. O'Connor said the applicant's "likely contributions to the intellectual and social life of the institution" should be considered an important factor in the admissions process.

The U.S. Supreme Court therefore found that race could continue to be one of many issues a college considered in its effort to ensure diversity on campus, which the court said was most important for the future intellectual development of young people. O'Connor—the first woman to serve on the U.S. Supreme Court—wrote, "In order to cultivate a set of leaders with legitimacy in the eyes of the citizenry, it is necessary that the path to leadership be open to talented and qualified individuals of every race and ethnicity."

Glossary

AFFIRMATIVE ACTION PROGRAMS—programs that are intended to improve the educational or employment opportunities of members of minority groups and women.

ATHEIST—a person who believes there is no God.

BIRACIAL—of, relating to, or involving members of two races.

DISCRIMINATION—prejudiced outlook, action, or treatment, often negative.

DIVERSE—composed of distinct or unlike elements or qualities, such as students from different racial and/or ethnic backgrounds.

FUNDAMENTALIST—beliefs based on a strict biblical interpretation of religious law.

INTERRACIAL DATING—a relationship involving two people of different races.

JIM CROW LAWS—laws established in the southern states following the Civil War that discriminated against African Americans and ensured racial segregation.

KWANZAA—a seven-day holiday celebrating African heritage that is observed in December.

LATINO—a person of Latin American origin living in the United States.

LINGUISTIC—relating to the development of language.

MEDIAN—in statistics, the number that falls in the center of a group, meaning half the numbers are higher and half are lower.

MINORITY—a part of a population different from the majority in some characteristics and often subjected to differential treatment.

MOSQUE—a place where Muslims worship.

MULTIRACIAL—of, relating to, or involving members of more than one race.

PLAINTIFF—a person making a complaint in a legal case in civil court.

Glossary

PRECEDENT—a legal ruling that sets an example for future laws and regulations.

PREJUDICE—an irrational attitude of hostility directed against an individual, a group, or a race.

QUOTA—percentage or share of a total that is made up of specific people or items, usually established by a rule or policy.

QUR'AN—the sacred scripture of Islam, which contains revelations made to Muhammad by Allah.

RACIAL PROFILING—projecting the characteristics of a few people onto the entire population of a group; for example, when police officers stop people on suspicion of criminal activity solely because of their race.

RACISM—discrimination against a particular group of people based solely on their racial background.

SEGREGATION—the separation or isolation of a race, class, or group from others in society. This can include restricting areas in which members of the race, class, or group can live; placing barriers to social interaction; establishing separate educational facilities; or other discriminatory means.

Internet Resources

http://www.gallup.com

The Gallup Organization's World Wide Web page features information of the Gallup Youth Surveys as well as the other polling work conducted by the organization.

http://www.census.gov

The U.S. Census Bureau has made available statistics on its World Wide Web site that reflect how the population of America is growing and changing, particularly when it comes to race. To learn about issues involving race, students can access information by going to the "Minority Links" section on the agency's home page.

http://www.splcenter.org

The Southern Poverty Law Center is dedicated to exposing hate groups and the crimes they commit. The organization makes many of its reports; as well as current news stories about hate crimes, available on its Internet site.

http://www.pbs.org/childofcamp

Companion World Wide Web site to the PBS documentary *Children of the Camps*, which examined the history of internment of Japanese Americans during World War II. The site includes a timeline, texts of historical documents, eyewitness accounts, and an examination of the physical and mental trauma suffered by the internees.

http://www.ed.gov

Many reports on diversity in American schools can be found at the World Wide Web site maintained by the U.S. Department of Education. The department's annual reports, titled "The Condition of Education," which contain the agency's views on how schools respond to issues of race, can be downloaded.

Internet Resources

http://www.pbs.org/wgbh/pages/frontline/shows/race

Companion World Wide Web site to the PBS documentary *The Two Nations of Black America*. This documentary examined the evolution of black society in the United States after the Civil Rights movement of the 1960s. The site includes economic data on the status of black Americans, an essay by Harvard professor Henry Louis Gates Jr., and interviews with black leaders, including Eldridge Cleaver, Angela Davis, Julian Bond, Cornel West, and Jesse Jackson.

http://www.islam101.com

World Wide Web site of the Sabr Foundation, which encourages understanding of Islam. The site includes a history of the Muslim people, an online introductory course for young people interested in studying Islam, and writings of Islamic scholars on such topics as human rights, women's issues, art, archaeology, and the Qur'an.

http://www.us-english.org
http://www.aclu.org

The debate over whether English should be the official language of the United States can be examined on the World Wide Web sites maintained by US English Inc., which supports the "English Only" policy, and the American Civil Liberties Union, which opposes it.

Publisher's Note: The websites listed in this book were active at the time of publication. The publisher is not responsible for websites that have changed their address or discontinued operation since the date of publication. The publisher reviews and updates the websites each time the book is reprinted.

Further Reading

Ferriss, Susan, and Ricardo Sandoval. *The Fight in the Fields: Cesar Chavez and the Farmworkers Movement.* New York: Harcourt Brace and Company, 1997.

Kitwana, Bakari. *The Hip Hop Generation: Young Blacks and the Crisis in African-American Culture.* New York: Basic Civistas Books, 2002.

Lester, Joan Steinau. *Fire in My Soul: The Biography of Eleanor Holmes Norton.* New York: Atria Books, 2003.

Tatum, Beverly Daniel. *Why Are All the Black Kids Sitting Together in the Cafeteria?* New York: Basic Books, 1997.

Wormser, Richard. *Growing Up Muslim in America.* New York: Walker and Company, 1994.

Wu, Frank. *Yellow: Race in America Beyond Black and White.* New York: Basic Books, 2002.

Yancey, George A., and Sherelyn Whittum Yancey, eds. *Just Don't Marry One: Interracial Dating, Marriage, and Parenting.* Valley Forge, Pa.: Judson Press, 2003.

Index

affirmative action, **86**, 88–99, **100**, 101
African Americans, 10, **11**, 13, 19–23,
    25–27, 29, **30**, 31–35, **41**
        See also segregation
American Civil Liberties Union (ACLU), 35,
    54, 74–75
American Civil Rights Institute, 98
anti-miscegenation laws, 52–54
        See also interracial marriage
Asians, 13, 23–24

Bakke, Alan, 90–92, 95, 99, 101
        See also affirmative action
Barnett, Ross, 26
Berry, Halle, 51
bilingual education. *See* education
biracial marriage. *See* interracial marriage
blacks. *See* African Americans
Blum, Edward, 98
Bowen, ReVonda, 38–40
Boyd, Ralph, 35
Bradley, Maime, **41**
Branch, Michelle, 51
Brown, Linda, 20
Brown v. Board of Education, **16**, 17, 20,
    22, 26, 30, 38, 89
        See also desegregation
Brownell, Herbert, 20
Bryant, Roy, **41**
Bush, George W., 35, 78, 85, 95
Bush, Jeb, 97
busing, 28–29, 32
        See also education

Carey, Mariah, 51
Census Bureau. *See* U.S. Census Bureau
Center for Equal Opportunity, 98
Central High School, 20–23
        See also desegregation

Chiu, Kenneth, 17
City University, 80
Civil Rights Act of 1964, 88, 91
civil rights movement, 9, **27**, 30
Clegg, Roger, 98
Cohen, Bernard, 54
Coleman, Mary Sue, 95
cultural identity. *See* ethnic identity

Dawson, Rosario, 51
desegregation, 20–23, 26–27, 28–32, 37
        See also Brown v. Board of Education;
        segregation
Diesel, Vin, 51
discrimination, 17–18, 23–26, 33–35, 39,
    40, **41**, 46–47, 71–73, 77–78, 85, 88
        See also racism; segregation
diversity (ethnic), **8**, 9–11, 13, 15, 32,
    92–93, 95
dropout rates, **30**, 65–67
        See also education

Eastside Journal, 25
Eckford, Elizabeth, 23
Edgeworth, Yvette, 55–56
education, **14**
    and affirmative action, 89–99, **100**,
        101
    college, 66, 67
    and language, **60**, 63–65, 68–71, **72**,
        74–75
    segregation and desegregation, **16**,
        17–23, 26–27, 28–32, 37, 46
        See also dropout rates
Eisenhower, Dwight D., 20, 21
Elmgreen, Sjon, 18
English. *See* language
"English Only" movement, 73–74
        See also language

Numbers in **bold italic** refer to captions and graphs.

Index

enrollment rates, 97, **99**
   See also education
Equal Employment Opportunity
   Commission (EEOC), 88
     See also affirmative action
ethnic identity, **48**, 49–50, 53, **58**
Executive Order 9066, 23–24
Executive Order 11246, 88–89, **90**
Executive Order 99-281, 97

Faubus, Orval, 20–21
Fordson High School, 81–82
Foster, Grant, 63–64

Gallup Youth Survey
   affirmative action, 96
   interracial dating, 41–42
   interracial marriage, 56–57
   Limited-English Proficient Programs,
     70–71
   race, 10
   terrorism, 84–85
     See also polls
Garrity, Arthur, 28–29
George Mason University, 63, 64
Grant Community School, 61, 63–64, 69,
   75
     See also education
Gratz, Jennifer, 93–94, 98–99, 101
     See also affirmative action
Grutter, Barbara, 94–95, 98, 101
     See also affirmative action

Hamacher, Patrick, 93–94, 98–99, 101
     See also affirmative action
Harris, David, 34–35
Harvard University, 30–32
Hatchett, Elaine, 47
higher education, 66, 67
     See also education

Hispanic Americans, 11, 15, **30**, 31–34
   discrimination against, 24–25, 71, 73
   and education, **62**, 63–71, **72**
Hood, James, 26
Hopwood, Cheryl, 96–97
Hughes, Van and Shirley, 52–53
Humphries, Hulond, 38–40
Husain, Altaf, 83
Hyde Park High School, 29
   See also busing

immigrants
   Asians, 23–24, 71
   Eastern European, 71
   Hispanic, 11–12, 25, 61, **62**, 63,
     67–68, 71
   Middle Eastern, 79–80
integration. *See* desegregation
internment camps, 23–24
interracial dating, **36**, 38, 41–44, **45**, 49
interracial marriage, 42, **48**, 49–51,
   52–57
interracial teens, 57–59
Islam. *See* Muslim Americans
Israeli-Palestinian conflict, 83

Jeter, Derek, 51, **55**
Jeter, Mildred. *See* Loving, Mildred
Jim Crow laws, 52
   See also anti-miscegenation laws
Johnson, Dwayne (The Rock), 51
Johnson, Lyndon B., 88–89, **90**

Kennedy, John F., 26–27, 88
Kennedy, Robert, 54
Keys, Alicia, 51
Knight, Delilah, 40
Kolbo, Kirk, 95
Kravitz, Lenny, 51

Index

language, **60**, 63–65, 68–71, **72**, 73–75
   See also education
Latinos, 15
   See also Hispanic Americans
Limited-English Proficient Programs, 69–71, 74
    See also education
Loving, Mildred, 53–54
Loving, Richard, 53–54
   See also anti-miscegenation laws

Malone, Vivian, 26
Marist College, 95–96
Marshall, Thurgood, 20
Martelli, Rose, 53
Martinez, Jorge, 71
Meredith, James, 26
Mexico, 11, 24–25
Milam, J. W., **41**
military, 55–56
   See also interracial marriage
Milliken v. Bradley, 29–30, 32
   See also education
minority populations, 10–11, 13, 15
Mujica, Mauro E., 74
multiracial households, 9–10, 50–51
   See also interracial marriage
Murray, Dennis, 96
Muslim Americans, 35, **76**, 77–83, **84**, 85
Muslim Students Association, 83
   See also Muslim Americans
Mya, 51

National Association for the Advancement of Colored People (NAACP), 47
"A National Study of School Effectiveness for Language Minority Students," 63
   See also education
Norton, Eleanor Holmes, 18–19

O'Connor, Sandra Day, 101
Orfield, Gary, 31

Patrick, Deval L., 39
Pennsylvania State University, 17–18
Plessy v. Ferguson, 19–20
   See also segregation
polls
   affirmative action, 95–96, **100**
   interracial marriage, 42
   Islam, **84**
   job opportunities, **12**
   language, **72**
   race relations, **14**
   racism, 34
   segregation, **22**
    See also Gallup Youth Survey
population
   minority, 10–11, 13, 15
   Muslim American, 78–80, **82**
   prison, 33–35
   U.S., 12, 50–51, 54–55
Posey, Erin, 47
prison population, 33–35
Proposition 209, **62**, 97, 99
   See also immigrants
protests, 25–26, **27**, 29

quota system, 92, 101
   See also affirmative action
Qur'an, 81
   See also Muslim Americans

racial profiling, 33–35
   See also discrimination
racism, 17–18, **24**, 34, 47, 59
   See also discrimination
Ramadan, 81
   See also Muslim Americans
Randolph County High School, 37–40

Index

Rehnquist, William, 99, 101
reverse discrimination, *91*, 96
   See also affirmative action
Richardson, Joshua, 33
Robinson, Vicky Sue, 51
The Rock (Dwayne Johnson), 51
Roosevelt, Franklin D., 23

Sabr Foundation, 80
   See also Muslim Americans
segregation, 26
school, *16*, 17–20, 26–27, *28*, 31–32, 46
   See also desegregation
"separate but equal" doctrine, 19–20, 37
   See also segregation
September 11, 2001. *See* terrorism
Sie, John, *76*
sit-ins. *See* protests
"some other race" designation, 15
   See also U.S. Census Bureau
South Boston High, 29
   See also busing
Spanish. *See* language
Spanish-American War, 24–25
Sterglas, Jeff, 82
Supreme Court. *See* U.S. Supreme Court
Swarthmore College, 93

Tatum, Beverly Daniel, 50, 53
Taylor County High School, 46–47
Teen Empowerment, 33
terrorism, 35, *76*, 77, *79*, 83, 84–85
Till, Emmett, 40, *41*
Tomas Rivera Policy Institute, 66
"two or more races" designation, 13, 50,
   51, 54–55, 56
      See also U.S. Census Bureau

University of Alabama, 26–27, *28*

University of California at Berkeley, *99*
University of California at Davis, 90–92
University of Michigan, 93–95, 96, 98–99
   See also affirmative action
University of Mississippi, 26
University of Missouri, 19–20
University of Texas, 96–97
University of Washington, 57
Ursinus College, 87–88, 92
U.S. Census Bureau, 10–13, 15, 50, *51*,
   54–55, 56, 61, 67, 69–70, 71, 73, 78
U.S. Department of Education, 32, 64–66,
   68, 69, 70, 90
U.S. English, 74
   See also "English Only" movement
U.S. Justice Deparment, 33, 35, 38–39,
   71, 73
U.S. Supreme Court, 28, 37, 53–54
   and affirmative action, 88, 91–92, *94*,
      95, 98–99, 101
   and *Brown v. Board of Education*, *16*,
      17, 20, *22*, 26, 30, 38, 89
   and *Milliken v. Bradley*, 29–30, 32
   and *Plessy v. Ferguson*, 19–20
U.S. Voting Rights Act, 71

Valdez, Eric, 18
Vickers, Nancy, 93
Villa, Pancho, 25

Wallace, George, 26–27, *28*
Waxman, Al, 25
whites, 10, 13, 15, 29, *30*, 31–32, 34
Wilson, Woodrow, 25
Woods, Tiger, *55*, 56
World War II, 23

"Zoot-Suit Riots," 25
   See also Hispanic Americans

Picture Credits

3: Corbis Images
8: ImageState
11: ImageState
12: © OTTN Publishing
14: © OTTN Publishing
16: Hulton/Archive/Getty Images
21: Hulton/Archive/Getty Images
22: Chart/Graph
24: Library of Congress [Prints and Photographs Division Reproduction # 276]
27: Hulton/Archive/Getty Images
28: Hulton/Archive/Getty Images
30: Corbis Images
34: © OTTN Publishing
36: Corbis Images
41: Bettmann/Corbis
42: PhotoDisc, Inc.
45: Corbis Images
48: Corbis Images
51: U.S. Census Bureau, United States Department of Commerce
55: (left) Scott Halleran/Getty Images
55: (right) Chris Trotman/Getty Images
58: Corbis Images
60: Corbis Images
62: Kim Kulish/Corbis Saba
65: ImageState
69: Mario Villafuerte/Getty Images
72: © OTTN Publishing
76: Manny Ceneta/Getty Images
79: United States Navy Photo
81: Erich Lessing/Art Resource, NY
82: Stephen Chernin/Getty Images
84: © OTTN Publishing
86: Corbis Images
90: Lyndon B. Johnson Presidential Library
91: Bettmann/Corbis
94: Najilah Feanny/Corbis Saba
99: Lara Jo Regan/Liaison/Getty Images
100: © OTTN Publishing

Cover: (front) Digital Vision; (back) ImageState

Contributors

GEORGE GALLUP JR. is chairman of The George H. Gallup International Institute (sponsored by The Gallup International Research and Education Center, or GIREC) and is senior scientist and member of the GIREC council. Mr. Gallup serves as chairman of the board of the National Coalition for Children's Justice and as a trustee of the National Fatherhood Initiative. He serves on many other boards in the area of health, education and religion.

Mr. Gallup is recognized internationally for his research and study on youth, health, religion, and urban problems. He has written numerous books including *My Kids On Drugs?* with Art Linkletter (Standard, 1981), *The Great American Success Story* with Alec Gallup and William Proctor (Dow Jones-Irwin, 1986), *Growing Up Scared in America* with Wendy Plump (Morehouse, 1995), *Surveying the Religious Landscape: Trends in U.S. Beliefs* with D. Michael Lindsay (Morehouse, 1999), and *The Next American Spirituality* with Timothy Jones (Chariot Victor Publishing, 1999).

Mr. Gallup received his BA degree from the Princeton University Department of Religion in 1954, and holds seven honorary degrees. He has received many awards, including the Charles E. Wilson Award in 1994, the Judge Issacs Lifetime Achievement Award in 1996, and the Bethune-DuBois Institute Award in 2000. Mr. Gallup lives near Princeton, New Jersey, with his wife, Kingsley. They have three grown children.

THE GALLUP YOUTH SURVEY was founded in 1977 by Dr. George Gallup to provide ongoing information on the opinions, beliefs and activities of America's high school students and to help society meet its responsibility to youth. The topics examined by the Gallup Youth Survey have covered a wide range—from abortion to zoology. From its founding through the year 2001, the Gallup Youth Survey sent more than 1,200 weekly reports to the Associated Press, to be distributed to newspapers around the nation. Since January 2002, Gallup Youth Survey reports have been made available on a weekly basis through the Gallup Tuesday Briefing.

HAL MARCOVITZ is a Pennsylvania journalist. His other topics in the GALLUP YOUTH SURVEY series include sex, suicide, and family issues. He lives in Chalfont, Pennsylvania, with his wife, Gail, and daughters Ashley and Michelle.